T0299873

The Myth of Bureaucratic Neutrality

In a system discredited by political corruption, the notion of "bureaucratic neutrality" was presented during the Progressive era as strategy to restore legitimacy in government. However, bureaucratic neutrality also served as a barrier to equity in government. This book argues that neutrality is a myth that has been used as a means to oppress marginalized communities, largely disconnected from its origins within the field of public administration. A historical perspective of how the field has understood race and gender demonstrates how it has centered whiteness, masculinity, and heteronormativity in research and administrative practices, mistaking them for neutrality in public service.

Using a historically grounded positionality approach, the authors trace the myth of bureaucratic neutrality back to its origins and highlight how it has institutionalized inequity, both legally and culturally. Ultimately, the authors demonstrate that the only way to move toward equity is to understand how inequity has become institutionalized, and to constantly work to improve our systems and decision-making.

With constituents across the globe demanding institutional changes in government that will establish new practices and mediate generations of inequality, *The Myth of Bureaucratic Neutrality* is required reading for public administration scholars, practitioners, and students.

Shannon K. Portillo is associate dean for academic affairs for the KU Edwards Campus and School of Professional Studies and a professor in the School of Public Affairs and Administration at the University of Kansas. Her work explores how formal policies and informal social norms shape the work of public organizations. She is specifically interested in how racism and sexism impact organizations and workers' experiences both historically and currently. Community service is a core value. Dr. Portillo served as Co-Chair of Governor Laura Kelly's

Commission on Racial Equity and Justice and Chair of the Douglas County Board of County Commissioners.

Nicole M. Humphrey is an assistant professor in the Department of Political Science at the University of Miami. Her work utilizes organizational behavior concepts grounded in public management scholarship to gain insight into diversity and equity in public sector organizations

Domonic A. Bearfield is an associate professor in the School of Public Affairs and Administration at Rutgers University-Newark. His work examines ideas related to race, gender, and public sector personnel. He also has a keen interest in issues that impact local governments, as well as the history of American public administration.

The Myth of Bureaucratic Neutrality

An Examination of Merit and Representation

Shannon K. Portillo, Nicole Humphrey and Domonic A. Bearfield

Routledge
Taylor & Francis Group

NEW YORK AND LONDON

First published 2023
by Routledge
605 Third Avenue, New York, NY 10158

and by Routledge
4 Park Square, Milton Park, Abingdon, Oxon, OX14 4RN

Routledge is an imprint of the Taylor & Francis Group, an informa business

Library of Congress Cataloging-in-Publication Data
A catalog record for this title has been requested

ISBN: 9781032345604 (hbk)
ISBN: 9781032345598 (pbk)
ISBN: 9781003322795 (ebk)

DOI: 10.4324/9781003322795

Typeset in Times New Roman
by Newgen Publishing UK

Contents

Acknowledgments

The premise for this book was developed back in the spring and summer of 2017. Over the past five years, several people have contributed to this project. The willingness of those around us to provide support and feedback is what allowed us to complete this book. We are grateful to have the help of so many people.

Writing this book has been a large undertaking that we could not have done with the support of our colleagues, friends, and family. First, we would like to thank Jessica Sowa. She was the first person that suggested we should write a book stemming from our article, "The Myth of Bureaucratic Neutrality: Institutionalized Inequity in Local Government Hiring" in the Review of Public Personnel Administration. Without her encouragement, we may not have started writing this book.

A number of individuals and groups provided space for feedback on these ideas, and we are incredibly grateful. Members of the Consortium for Race and Gender Scholars hosted webinars and workshops where we gained valuable feedback. We are particularly grateful to Leisha Dehart-Davis, Staci Zavattaro, Susan Gooden, and Norma Riccucci for their early feedback on this project.

We would also like to thank our Editor, Laura Varley, and Editorial Assistants Katie Horsfall and Ella Halstead for their help throughout this process.

Shannon K. Portillo would like to thank her family. Mom and Dad (Jo and Jerry Portillo), you have always been in my corner, willing to stand up for me but also providing a strong foundation so I could learn to stand up for myself. My husband, Jevan Bremby, is a support through every up and down, consistently willing to discuss big issues (and small issues) in public service, politics, and local government over dinner (and breakfast, and before bed, and randomly as I wander into his office while working from home during a pandemic). I am excited to figure out life with you. I appreciate that you live your values everyday, and I am thrilled that you choose me.

I have been so fortunate to have friends in this field who continue to push me. Domonic and I *tried* to write together for the first time way back in 2008. We've pushed each other to think more deeply throughout our careers, but it turns out we needed Nicole to balance us out and force us to put ideas on paper. I am so grateful for how this collaboration has grown and remain excited for our future work. I started in my first tenure track job alongside Danielle Rudes. From day one we decided we'd lift each other up and always lift while we climb. She has brought so many amazing, supportive people into my life and my work through our Powerful Women's Dinners, I am sure I would not still be an academic if it wasn't for her. She inspires me to pay it forward as a mentor and I am grateful for every moment of it.

Nicole Humphrey would like to thank her parents, Carmela and Allen Humphrey. You have always provided me with love, support, and inspiration. I was lucky enough to grow up with parents who were the embodiment of dedication and care. I am thankful for all that you are, and all that you have done for me.

I would also like to thank my fiancé, Ashley. I always tell people you're the type of person that makes the world go round. Without you, I know that my life, and the life of so many other people, would not be filled with the same level of joy, goofiness, and unconditional love.

I would also like to give the biggest thank you to both of my coauthors, Shannon and Domonic. I can't imagine working in academia without the two of you. You both have been constant pillars of support, and I'm grateful to have you in my corner.

Domonic Bearfield would like to thank Shannon K. Portillo and Nicole Humphrey, the two best co-authors that anyone could ever ask for. I am a better writer, scholar, and friend because of the two of you. At various points throughout this project, I have been lifted up by your collective patience, determination, curiosity, and intellect. I can't believe that our conference conversations forged a collaboration that now spans multiple projects – including this book. We have literally learned how to finish each other's sentences. I am eternally grateful for both of you.

To my mentor Melvin J. Dubnick. Since day one, you have pushed, encouraged, and supported my journey as a scholar. Thanks for reading DuBois and engaging me when everyone wondered why anyone would care about patronage. The push to question the myths of our field comes from you.

Ann Bowman, Jennifer Brinkerhoff, Khalilah L. Brown-Dean, Warren Eller, Madinah Hamidullah, Alisa Hicklin, Ken Meier, Charles Menifield, Lindsey McDougle, Jeryl Mumpower, Sanjay Pandey, Michael Pennington, Ellen Rubin, Dan Smith, Adeyemi Stembridge, Quincy Thomas Stewart, Edward Tarlton, Omar Wandera, and James Wright. Thank you for your thoughts, comments, and questions on early drafts, conference presentations, and the articles related to this project. Your input has been invaluable.

I want to say, "Behold!" to my Spartan family. Also, a special thank you to the men of the Epsilon Pi chapter of Alpha Phi Alpha Fraternity Inc. I have recited "Don't Quit" countless times while working on this book. I appreciated every text, phone call, and e-mail.

I am blessed to come from a family of public servants. My mother, Sharran Bearfield, spent part of her career at Head Start and with the Boy Scouts of America. My father, Alex Bearfield, is a retired police officer. My brother, Dorian, followed in my Dad's footsteps and is a police officer himself. Everything I know about the commitment and sacrifice required to serve the public results from the lessons you have shared with me. You are the inspiration for this book.

And finally, I want to thank my amazing wife and partner, Rachel Emas. Thank you for all your help and support, especially during the final months of this project. You are the living embodiment of the phrase "I got you." I lack the words to tell you how much I appreciate your thoughtfulness, intelligence, determination, and kindness. Just know that I am in awe of you, and I know I would not have been able to finish this book without you.

1 Introduction

The idea for this book was born out of shared frustration. As graduate students, each of us ran into a moment where the reality presented in the literature on topics related to equity, identity, and discrimination did not match our lived experience. For one of us, it was discovering that the information we learned about patronage – that the process of hiring based on political connections was inherently corrupt and could not be tolerated – did not reflect the experience of African American public sector workers. During the Progressive Era, many African Americans who gained their employment through the patronage system had little faith that the shift to the merit system – an examination-based hiring system – would treat them fairly, despite the fact that they were more than qualified for their positions (Portillo, Bearfield, & Humphrey, 2019).

For another, it was recognition that beneath verbal claims of neutrality from key actors during the field's genesis were often actions that promoted injustice. For instance, while local governments hired professional administrators to prove their commitment to the concepts of neutrality and fairness (Montjoy & Watson, 1995), they also took direct action to minimize the participation of women and people of color in their communities. Through actions like employment discrimination and segregation, governments, claiming to be fair and neutral, were acting in ways that directly contradicted these statements.

Lastly, one of us came to realize the mismatch between the literature and lived experiences of marginalized communities via the courts. Landmark civil rights cases of the mid-twentieth century promised to implement American ideals in equitable ways. However, the reality of housing, school, and employment inequity in the early twenty-first century, challenged these concepts. Exploring how employees in public organizations understood the rules and laws that governed their work (Portillo, 2012) made it clear that concepts of equity were still far from the reality of the modern workplace. In short, while rules promised

DOI: 10.4324/9781003322795-1

neutrality, they are often implemented in ways that reinforced existing power hierarchies.

In each case, the literature asked us to put our faith in objective systems and administrators, even though as scholars, we knew that many of these systems were far from neutral. In fact, as we deepened our understanding, it became clear that in some instances greater inequality was actually the goal of some *neutral* systems – disparities in treatment were not a misstep or mistake, but the core objective. Throughout our careers, as we have engaged with other scholars who identify as women, queer, and people of color. During these interactions, we noticed that we were not alone in our frustration with public administration literature. While the ideals of bureaucratic neutrality were always prominent, the lack of critique on the concept rarely sat well with us.

It would be cynical to say that we were lied to. Nor does that accurately capture what happened. Those around us did not intentionally mislead us. In fact, they were largely passing down the same lessons that were taught to them. Instead, we became immersed in one of the living myths of public administration – that science will save us from evil. And, because of this, we should lean into neutral bureaucratic systems that implement administrative practices based on scientific evidence without questioning how these practices might reinforce inequity. In this book, we will explore the concept of bureaucratic neutrality in an attempt to understand administrative actions that reinforce inequity. Specifically, we will address several myths in the field of public administration with a focus on three areas: merit, representation, and legal remedies. We argue that, for a variety of reasons, discrimination does implicitly and explicitly impact administrative decision-making. In some cases, the discriminatory effect is isolated or individualistic. However, in other cases, like segregation laws or Jim Crow, it is more pervasive and systemic. We will also explain why our current approaches to discussing discrimination and inequity in American bureaucracies are insufficient and propose a new approach that more accurately integrates discussions of our past into our present. Throughout this book, we will discuss the myths that have permeated the field of public administration, and how we might dismantle those myths and move forward with a more critical approach to research and practice.

Recovering from the Flood

During the initial discussions for this project, we discovered a connection between floods and myths as a source of inspiration. For instance, after a great flood, it is common for writers, artists, and others to examine the aftermath in search of meaning. Floods often represents a time for cleansing, where the wickedness has been washed away, and structures, cities, and traditions can start anew. There are other times when we look at the flood to examine how things could go so wrong. As we look at the wreckage, we see our faults and vulnerabilities. The missed opportunities to protect the things that we hold dear.

On August 23, 2005, a category five hurricane hit (near and around) the state of Louisiana. The city of New Orleans was particularly devastated by the storm as much of the city sat underwater for days. Houses were flooded. People had to be evacuated from their rooftops. And the searing images of families living on the New Orleans superdome struck a chord with many Americans. It was hard to overlook that so many of the families left behind were Black. In fact, slow federal response became synonymous with Black pain in these communities.

Hurricane Katrina was a galvanizing event, so it is no surprise that many scholars turned to this catastrophe in search of meaning. In the months following Hurricane Katrina, after witnessing the destruction and devastation caused by the storm, Camilla Stivers (2007) questioned if racism played a role in the response. She noted that some decisions, if taken in isolation, could be the result of individual bureaucratic mistakes. However, she also highlighted that we cannot ignore that race may have played a factor in the response to a city often seen as poor and Black.

The image of flooding reminded us of a parable described by Stewart and Ray (2007) as the race flood. In the allegory, racism acts like a flood that damages every house that it comes in contact with. And, even after the flood waters recede, the house is still filled with toxins that can cause the residents of the contaminated houses to become sick, even though the water is no longer there. In their scenario, the flood represents racism, and the houses are institutions that have been contaminated by the flood. While they used this story to describe differences in health outcomes, it is important to consider how this story can apply to other forms of discrimination (e.g., sexism, homophobia, transphobia, xenophobia).

It is also necessary to consider how this tale contains lessons for public administration. While policy makers have won many hard-fought victories toward addressing racism, sexism, homophobia and other forms of discrimination (draining the flood), our institutions are still stained by the legacy of those practices. Recovering from a flood is no easy task. Ridding out contamination is work that must extend to each and every part of our institutions (the houses). While formal discrimination is no longer tolerated (there is no more water in the house), the remnants are still affecting the structures of our field (the toxins from the flood remain in the house). These remnants are maintained through myths that help rationalize their existence. Our purpose is to bring these myths to light, so that we can recover from the flood.

Myths, Not Lies

Given the complexity of the world around us, myths are tools we use to help make sense of things. Grant (1998) notes that myths "represent a web of visions and loyalties that give life shape and meaning" (p. IX). Often, people tend to think of myths as lies. But that is not necessarily the case. They are a way to chronicle our triumphs, failures, and mysteries in narrative form. At times, they are an oversimplification of complex ideas. At other times, the myths themselves are intricate and complex.

In the context of organizations, myths help to develop legitimacy and align an organization with societal norms and values (Portillo, Bearfield, & Humphrey, 2019; Meyer & Rowan, 1997; Tolbert & Zucker, 1983). Within the context of public administration scholarship and practice, we often not only see the presence of myths, but rationalized myths. Rationalized myths are a concept grounded in literature on institutionalism (Frederickson, Smith, Larimer, & Licari, 2015; March & Olsen, 1989; Portillo & Humphrey, 2018). They describe "widespread social understandings that may manifest in policies or practices that are effectively taken for granted as the right way to adapt and function" (Portillo, Bearfield, & Humphrey, 2019, p. 521). Rationalized myths are ideas so taken for granted they become nearly invisible as myths and are assumed to be shared knowledge.

As a field, public administration has a series of myths that we tell ourselves. For instance, there are competing myths surrounding the role of science in the field. In one version, it is the triumph of the quantitative methods, i.e., research approaches using statistical analysis, over qualitative approaches. Yet, qualitative scholars will argue that quantitative approaches have done little to advance our knowledge on the reality of public service work, and instead seek to answer more narrow questions because that is where the data are found. Neither of these statements captures the complexity of the different approaches to the field. In fact, the relationship between quantitative and qualitative approaches has been far more symbiotic than either scholarly community would care to admit. But, the tales allow members of each community to engage in a triumphant narrative over the other. And, and in turn, they are able to celebrate their success and to attract new members. In our cases, we were told to put our faith in the belief that objective administrators and examinations could be used to improve the lives for a host of communities that we deeply cared about.

American public administration and the administrative state often find their roots in the Progressive Era (Stivers, 1995). The Progressive Era roughly took place between the late-1800s and 1920 (Lee, 2011). As Mosher (1982) reminds us, Progressive reformers were largely engaged in a moral battle of good versus evil, with concerns about efficiency a distant second. As reformers sought to reclaim their cities from moral decline, they turned to a belief in the scientific method as one of the tools. From this emerged the idea of the neutral bureaucrat, or the concept of bureaucratic neutrality, and with it the belief that individuals who serve the public would, to use a modern term, simply follow the science, without concerns for external political pressure or their individual bias.

In and of itself, the idea of a neutral administrator, or the belief that decisions will be made without concern for bias or favor, is an important normative idea – it is also a myth. One that has been handed down, generation by generation, to scholars and practitioners alike. In practice, it has been revealed that administrators, and the systems they create, can be infused with much of the prejudice and discrimination that bureaucratic neutrality was supposed to eliminate. It is not enough to lean on the explanatory power of our old myths. Now is the time to push further – to address the myths that have been overlooked in our field and to apply a more critical approach that utilizes our field's history to make more equitable decisions in the present.

Defining Bureaucratic Neutrality

Bureaucratic neutrality is an idealized characteristic of public servants commonly promoted and pursued by public administration scholars and practitioners. Furthermore, bureaucratic neutrality is often discussed along two dimensions. The first dimension emphasizes public servants who are uninfluenced by politics. This was a notion initially promoted at the outset of the field with the politics-administration dichotomy (Wilson, 1887; Goodnow, 1900). To prevent corruption in the business of government, public administrators needed to be separated from politics (Rosenbloom, 2001). The second dimension of bureaucratic neutrality is a broader notion embedded in the belief that the government should pursue the ideals of efficiency, rationality, and objectivity. Scholars that helped shape the field during this time promoted the idea of public administration becoming a "design science" (Rosenbloom, 2001). Their desire was for the field to emphasize an identity that focused on professional standards and technical ability (Green, Wamsley, & Kell, 1993), so public administration would be considered a profession. As such, one of the goals of early practitioners and scholars was to increase the legitimacy of the field by focusing on the technical nature of the work, and the relationship to science and objectivity.

We can see the pursuit of bureaucratic neutrality throughout the United States' different levels of government. For instance, at the federal level practitioners began extensive civil service reform through the Pendleton Act of 1883. The Pendleton Act possessed three core standards meant to professionalize the civil service and promote bureaucratic neutrality within the federal government:

> (1) It provided that admission to the federal service be based on open, competitive testing; (2) it prohibited firing federal employees for any reason other than cause; and (3) it provided that no political pressure or coercion be exerted on federal employees for contributions or specific actions.
>
> (Ingraham, 2006, p. 486)

With these three tenets, the Pendleton Act of 1883 formally established the civil service merit system and diminished opportunities for corruption and wrongdoing through the spoils system (providing contracts or employment based on political connections rather than merit) (Ingraham, 2006; Woodard, 2005).

Along with changes at the federal level, there were also notable reforms happening in local government to promote bureaucratic neutrality. The year 1908 marked the appointment of the nation's first city manager in Staunton, Virginia (Montjoy & Watson, 1995; Stillman, 2014). Richard Childs, a notable advocate for reforming local government, heard of the appointment in Staunton and began to develop a new plan for municipal government that would incorporate a professional manager into prior forms of government (Stillman, 2014). In 1915, the National Municipal League adopted Childs' plan that is now commonly referred to as the council-manager form of government (Montjoy & Watson, 1995). In addition to the council-manager form of government, municipalities also began to adopt merit-based hiring practices, similar to federal practices. While the Pendleton Act did not require municipal governments to partake in civil service reform, policies in the act were still reflected at the local level (Portillo, Bearfield, & Humphrey, 2019).

Collectively, the reforms of this era were meant to bring bureaucratic neutrality to government administration as a means to prevent continued patronage and political corruption through a technocratic emphasis that minimized the influence of partisan politics and promoted skill and expertise (Rosenbloom, 2008). With scholars holding up bureaucratic neutrality as the savior of U.S. governance during the Progressive Era, neutrality quickly became a defining characteristic of the field of public administration. While the field has historically used bureaucratic neutrality to convey impartiality and rational behavior, it often fails to acknowledge how bureaucratic neutrality has embedded whiteness and masculinity into the field of public administration (Portillo, Humphrey, & Bearfield, 2022).

The Public Administration Identity

At the outset of the Progressive Era, we see race playing a key role in the reform movement. Specifically, while reformers wanted to end the spoils system that apportioned government contracts and employment based on political connections, they were also deeply concerned with demographic changes due to immigration (Rosenbloom, 2008). Previous scholarship has suggested that "a large source of external legitimacy for the civil service reform was related to an increase in nativism and anti-immigrant sentiment" (Portillo, Bearfield, & Humphrey, 2019, p. 523), meaning race and whiteness were central to the development of the administrative state. This suggests that reformers of the time were not just concerned with minimizing political influence or developing a profession, they were also concerned with maintaining power for native-born, white Americans in government. One method of maintaining this power was through policies and structures often described as neutral.

While neutrality has ties to race, it also has clear ties to gender. As Stivers (1995, 2002) explains, men of the Progressive Era connected masculinity with the ideals of scientific management – efficiency and rationality. With men interested in reform often being called unmanly for wanting to end the spoils system, they leaned on concepts of science and rationality as a means to protect and legitimize their masculinity (Stivers, 1995). This suggests that while bureaucratic neutrality helped end corruption in government, it also helped preserve the masculine identity of government administration.

Central to understanding public administration in the United States is understanding the concepts of race, gender, whiteness, and masculinity. While historically absent from explicit discussions on the genesis of the field, race and gender both had a notable influence on the development of public administration. At the foundation of our field, key actors sought to preserve whiteness and masculinity, allowing these characteristics to be used as a benchmark of what constitutes a public servant. Whiteness and masculinity have therefore become entangled with our understanding of neutrality. Entangling these qualities with neutrality reinforces the inequities of marginalized groups that fail to meet the social demographic characteristics associated with public service.

We, as scholars and practitioners, have influenced how race, gender, and other identities are constructed and treated in the field of public administration (Yanow, 2003). At the same time, we often do not recognize how we have done this and the lasting impact it has on public administration research and practice. By failing to acknowledge our role in allowing whiteness and masculinity to become embedded in the field of public administration, we are giving continued life to biased practices and beliefs. Our purpose in this book is to gain a deep understanding of biases present in the field of public administration by examining commonly held myths that have helped reinforce inequity, while also presenting historically grounded positionality as a new approach to understand and examine equity. Historically grounded positionality asks us to consider how the past continues to influence decision-making and practices currently. It provides a framework to understand how the rationalized myths of our founding are still here today and how we might change them and move toward more equitable practices in our field.

Summary of Book

Chapter 1 has been used to highlight the overarching concept of bureaucratic neutrality. The remaining chapters build on this discussion, emphasizing other notable myths in public administration, and how we can begin to dismantle these myths in our scholarship and practice.

The following chapter examines the concept of identity in public administration. Identity is an elusive concept, but a topic of the utmost importance since it is central to understanding the lived experiences of public employees and those that they serve. To address the topic of identity, Chapter 2 explores common identity frameworks in public administration scholarship – race, gender, and heteronormativity. In addition, this chapter discusses the importance of intersectionality as a means to study multiple intersecting identities, while also proposing historically grounded positionality as an additional framework to supplement the field's understanding of identity in public organizations.

Chapter 3 analyzes another common myth in the field of public administration – the myth of merit. Similar to the concept of bureaucratic neutrality, public administration scholars and practitioners have often held the concept of merit in high esteem. However, it is important to consider how merit is connected to the concept of identity in the public sector workforce. In this chapter, we argue that perceived bureaucratic neutrality of merit-based hiring at the local, state, and federal levels of government continues to permeate public administration practice and scholarship with profound implications for discussions of equity and social justice. Using an institutional framework, this chapter demonstrates how merit-based hiring is often a rationalized myth – meaning that rationale is often disconnected from the purpose. Specifically, we explore how the concept of merit has evolved over time, and how changes in our expectations of merit have at times been a detriment to marginalized communities.

In the following substantive chapter, Chapter 4, we examine the myth of representation. In the field of public administration, representative bureaucracy assumes bureaucratic organizations that reflect their constituents will reflect the interests of those constituents (Krislov, 1974; Meier, Wrinkle, & Polinard, 1999). While we agree with the core assumption of representative bureaucracy, we take aim at how this area of literature often overlooks how whiteness and masculinity are often absent from our discussions of representative bureaucracy. Specifically, representative bureaucracy literature too narrowly focuses on how employees of color must be the ones to resolve inequity, without acknowledging that those belonging to historically dominant social identities must also pursue equity. This is the myth of representation – only bureaucrats of the same background can provide efficient, effective, and equitable services in diverse communities. The myth of representation masks inequalities built into bureaucratic organizations and places the burden of fixing these inequalities on bureaucrats who have historically been discriminated against.

Chapter 5 takes on the myth of legal remedies. The law has often been viewed as a remedy to social injustice and discrimination in the United States. However, history has shown that the law and the legal system alone, do not create social and organizational change, and written laws prohibiting discrimination do not guarantee there is no discrimination in practice. Our purpose in this chapter is to address this myth and explore the limits of the law as a remedy for discrimination. The chapter highlights how and why changes in law and policy alone will not fix historic inequities.

In Chapter 6, we shift course. Rather than continuing to analyze public administration myths that perpetuate inequity, we analyze the concept of historically grounded positionality as a means to study and practice public administration. Central to challenging institutionalized inequity in public administration is improving the field's understanding of identity. While public administration scholars have begun using intersectionality as a framework to understand identity (see Breslin, Pandey, & Riccucci, 2017 for a review), our work regularly falls short of fully realizing the complexities of identity in public organizations. More specifically, public administration often discusses identity as a static concept, overlooking that the way people interpret and perform their identities is constantly evolving. Intersectionality provides us with a frame to acknowledge that someone can possess more than one identity and experience multiple oppressions (Bearfield, 2009; Gaynor & Blessett, 2014; Blessett, 2018). However, solely relying on intersectionality as a frame to understand identity prevents scholars from seeing how identity and oppression transform over time and in different settings. To address this issue, we propose public administration scholarship that begins incorporating a historically grounded positionality approach to research. This approach incorporates intersectionality and acknowledges that geographic and temporal nuances shape how individuals and communities understand identity. Understanding how identity changes over time allows us to unmask the myths of our field and move toward more equitable decision-making and practices.

In the concluding chapter, Chapter 7, we expand on the concept of historically grounded positionality and provide explicit examples of how public administration can decenter whiteness, masculinity, and heteronormativity as a way to move toward inclusivity and equity. While bureaucracy is not neutral, it should strive to pursue the concepts of equity and fairness (Gooden, 2014). Historically grounded positionality highlights that dealing with inequity is a never-ending battle because inequity is not static. We are and will forever be pursuing a moving target. As the demographics of our communities change, governments at all levels are being called upon to evaluate their actions and ensure that their institutions are not further perpetuating inequity. To meet this expectation, public administration scholars and practitioners must become well-versed in the field's history and how we as scholars and practitioners have institutionalized inequity. It is only through understanding how the past shaped the present that we can move toward more equity in the future. Moving forward, a primary concern among public administration scholars and practitioners should be to improve how we study and manage inequity in the public sector.

Given the increasingly recognized importance of diversity and equity in public administration, our purpose is to address the myths that have created barriers in the field's pursuit of these concepts. Moving forward, we must change the narrative in public administration scholarship and practice, from one that accepts myths that reinforce inequity, to one that actively seeks to understand and challenge these myths. Overall, our hope is that by addressing commonly held myths, we can help the field of public administration take a more comprehensive and critical approach to diversity and equity in both research and practice.

Works Cited

Bearfield, D. A. (2009). Equity at the intersection: Public administration and the study of gender. *Public Administration Review*, *69*(3), 383–386.

Blessett, B. (2018). Rethinking the administrative state through an intersectional framework. *Administrative Theory & Praxis*, *42*(1), 1–5.

Breslin, R. A., Pandey, S., & Riccucci, N. M. (2017). Intersectionality in public leadership research: A review and future research agenda. *Review of Public Personnel Administration*, *37*(2), 160–182.

Frederickson, H. G., Smith, K. B., Larimer, C. W., & Licari, M. (2015). *The public administration theory primer* (3rd ed.). Westview Press.

Gaynor, T. S., & Blessett, B. (2014). Inequality at the intersection of the defense of marriage act and the voting rights act. *Administrative Theory & Praxis*, *36*(2), 261–267.

Gooden, S. (2014). *Race and social equity: A nervous area of government*. Sharpe.

Goodnow, F. J. (1900). *Politics and administration: A study in government*. Russell & Russell.

Grant, C. (1998). *Myths we live by*. University of Ottawa Press.

Green, R. T., Wamsley, G. L., & Keller, L. F. (1993). Reconstituting a profession for American public administration. *Public Administration Review*, *53*(6), 516–524.

Ingraham, P. W. (2006). Building bridges over troubled waters: Merit as a guide. *Public Administration Review*, *66*(4), 486–495.

Krislov, S. (1974). *Representative bureaucracy*. Prentice Hall.

Lee, M. (2011). History of US public administration in the Progressive Era: Efficient government by and for whom? *Journal of Management History*, *17*(1), 88–101.

March, J. G., & Olsen, J. P. (1989). *Rediscovering institutions: The organizational basis of politics*. Free Press.

Meier, K. J., Wrinkle, R. D., & Polinard, J. L. (1999). Representative bureaucracy and distributional equity: Addressing the hard question. *Journal of Politics*, *61*(4), 1025–1039.

Meyer, J. W., & Rowan, B. (1977). Institutionalized organizations: Formal structure as myth and ceremony. *American Journal of Sociology*, *83*(2), 340–363.

Montjoy, R. S., & Watson, D. J. (1995). A case for reinterpreted dichotomy of politics and administration as a professional standard in council-manager government. *Public Administration Review*, *55*(3), 231–239.

Mosher, F. C. (1982). *Democracy and the public service*. Oxford University Press.

Portillo, S. (2012). The paradox of rules: Rules as resources and constraints. *Administration & Society, 44*(1), 87–108.

Portillo, S., Bearfield, D., & Humphrey, N. (2019). The myth of bureaucratic neutrality: Institutionalized inequity in local government hiring. *Review of Public Personnel Administration, 40*(30), 516–531.

Portillo, S., & Humphrey, N. (2018). Institutionalism and assumptions: Institutionalizing race and gender in public administration scholarship. In E. C. Stazyk & H. G. Frederickson (Eds.), *Handbook of American public administration* (pp. 289–303). Edward Elgar Publishing.

Portillo, S., Humphrey, N., & Bearfield, D. A. (2022). Representative bureaucracy theory and the implicit embrace of whiteness & masculinity. *Public Administration Review, 82*(3), 594–597.

Rosenbloom, D. H. (2001). History lessons for reinventors. *Public Administration Review, 61*(2), 161–165.

———. (2008). The politics–administration dichotomy in US historical context. *Public Administration Review, 68*(1), 57–60.

Stewart, Q. T., & Ray, R. (2007). Hurricane Katrina and the race flood: Interactive lessons for quantitative research on race. *Race, Gender & Class, 14*(1/2), 38–59.

Stillman, R. (2014). 1914: Celebrating the centennial of ICMA and modern American government. *Public Management, 96*(8), 10–13.

Stivers, C. (1995). Settlement women and bureau men: Constructing a usable past for public administration. *Public Administration Review, 55*(6), 522–529.

———. (2007). "So poor and so black": Hurricane Katrina, public administration, and the issue of race. *Public Administration Review, 67*(1), 48–56.

Stivers, C. M. (2000). *Bureau men, settlement women: Constructing public administration in the Progressive Era.* University Press of Kansas.

Tolbert, P. S., & Zucker, L. G. (1983). Institutional sources of change in the formal structure of organizations: The diffusion of civil service reform, 1880–1935. *Administrative Science Quarterly, 28*(1), 22–39.

Wilson, W. (1887). The study of administration. *Political Science Quarterly, 2*(2), 197–222.

Woodard, C. A. (2005). Merit by any other name: Refraining the civil service first principle. *Public Administration Review, 65*(1), 109–116.

Yanow, D. (2003). *Constructing race and ethnicity in America: Category-making in public policy and administration.* Routledge.

2 Identity in Public Administration

Located on the eastern edge of Missouri, Saint Louis was a once thriving city, often referred to as the gateway to the west. In more recent times, scholars have described Saint Louis as a classic example of "urban decline" (Taylor, 2013, p. 183). The struggles of the city have been reflected in many of its public organizations, like the Saint Louis County Police Department. A notable challenge faced by the Saint Louis County Police Department is how to be inclusive of the various identities present among its officers. Within the context of public administration, identity is essential to understanding the experiences of public servants and constituents of public agencies. The ways in which our institutions perceive and treat someone's identity will have a notable impact on that person's lived experiences in society (House-Niamke & Eckerd, 2021). In addition, when organizations fail to be inclusive of the many identities present among their employees and the communities they serve, they will inevitably find themselves in hot water.

Within the last ten years, the Saint Louis County Police Department has had lawsuits filed against it with plaintiffs claiming the organization discriminated against them based on their gender, race, and sexual orientation. One of the most prominent lawsuits in the past few years involved Keith Wildhaber, a sergeant who joined the Saint Louis County Police Department in the mid-1990s (Treisman, 2019). Wildhaber was consistently passed over for promotions, even though his performance reviews showed that he was not only qualified for the positions that he was applying but also had a record of performance that went above department standards (Treisman, 2019). Wildhaber, who identifies as gay, attributed issues with his promotion to his sexuality. When John Saracino, a member of the Saint Louis County Board of Police Commissioners told Wildhaber, "The command staff has a problem with your sexuality. If you ever want to see a white shirt [i.e., get a promotion], you should tone down your gayness" (Treisman, 2019),

DOI: 10.4324/9781003322795-2

suspicions that the Department struggled with issues of discrimination based on sexual orientation were confirmed. In October of 2019, a jury awarded Wildhaber just over 19 million dollars in damages from the case (Treisman, 2019).

At its foundation, this is an issue of an organization not knowing how to be inclusive of an identity that has been historically othered. Wildhaber is part of the LGBTQ (i.e., Lesbian, Gay, Bisexual, Transgender, and Queer) community. While U.S. law enforcement has been viewed as "monolithically white, male, and straight" (Sklansky, 2005, p. 1210), recently the demographics of many departments has begun to change with greater representation of historically underrepresented groups (Donohue, 2020). However, as the Saint Louis County Police Department demonstrates, many local law enforcement agencies have struggled to adjust to changes in the ranks of their officers. While Wildhaber's case is arguably the most notable issue in the Department's recent history, the Saint Louis County Police Department has found itself in turmoil several other times due to its inability to be inclusive of all identities.

For another example, consider the former Chief of the Saint Louis County Police Department, Mary Barton. Chief Barton was appointed to lead a police department in a county with a long history of racial tensions. Saint Louis is a hyper-segregated area, "meaning that at least 60 percent of the white and black residents would have to move to a new census block to end segregation" (Benton, 2018, p. 1113). The racial divide in Saint Louis is often attributed to discriminatory policies that were focused on creating "racially isolated housing communities" during the mid-twentieth century (Taylor, 2013, p. 183). These practices from the last century are getting increasing scrutiny now as communities across the country discuss the lasting impacts of red lining. Unsurprisingly, the racial divide in the city has a lasting impact on local communities and is also mirrored in some public organizations, like the Police Department.

Discussions of race and racism must be central to solving issues of inequity within public sector organizations. While policies of the past that created racial divides may no longer be practiced, their ramifications are still present within public organizations. However, topics of race and racism represent a "nervous area" within the field of public administration (Gooden, 2014), which leads both scholars and practitioners to avoid discussing race and racism, and, by extension, the implications they have on public management.

Following the death of George Floyd in May 2020 at the hands of local police officers in Minneapolis, Minnesota (Van Oot & Van Berkel,

2020), many local police departments were tasked with acknowledging the racial tensions present within their communities and organizations. The Saint Louis County Police Department was no exception. At a Saint Louis County council meeting in June of 2020, Chief Barton said the department needed to shift its culture and, "no longer tolerate or no longer put up with inappropriate remarks, inappropriate behavior, things we deem unethical, [and] things we deem insensitive" (Lippmann, 2020). When Chief Barton was questioned on whether the inappropriate behavior previously seen in the department could be labeled as racism, she responded:

> Some of it is ageism, some of it is sexism. And I think to say that there's systemic racism in the police department is overly broad and probably not accurate. Until we sit down and talk about it and can verify or at least ferret out what it is people are talking about, I think to put a label on it is really unfair and shortsighted.
>
> (Lippmann, 2020)

A few days later, Chief Barton backpedaled on this comment, acknowledging racism was a topic her department needed to deal with (Lippmann, 2020). However, her initial response to discussions of racism in the Saint Louis County Police Department highlights how race continues to be a "nervous area of government" (Gooden, 2014). As such, race and racism become topics that people attempt to avoid. However, avoidance only entrenches these issues by attempting to make them invisible when they influence decision-making and practices within organizations.

Recognizing the many ways public organizations in the United States have sought to exclude individuals and groups from public arenas and government services based on social characteristics, it is apparent that discussions of fairness and neutrality in government were not always genuine. Scholars interested in exploring issues of fairness and neutrality in public administration have often taken an interdisciplinary approach and utilized research from other fields and disciplines, like sociology, law and society, history, Black, Latinx, gender, and queer studies, to find the answers that were not provided to us by the traditional public administration literature. Central in each of these literatures was the way individuals and communities perceived and treated identity.

In the field of public administration, we have studied identity and the outcomes of several identity groups. Recent examples include Sabharwal and colleagues' (2019) study of turnover intentions among LGBTQ employees, Funk's (2019) analysis of gender role congruity and the implications this concept has for the performance evaluations of women in managerial positions, as well as Smith and colleagues' (2020) exploration of workplace incivility as it relates to race and gender. However, we have not adequately connected the outcomes of marginalized groups with the actions of our administrative institutions. In this book, we attempt to incorporate discussions of identity from both the field of public administration and several other fields and disciplines, to make these connections that allow for a deeper understanding of how administrative institutions have impacted underrepresented groups. Our purpose is to explore how public administration has historically treated *different* identities, and the lasting implications of this treatment.

Social Equity as the Foundation

When considering how scholars began to study identity in public administration, it is helpful to begin with an exploration into the concept of social equity. While at its genesis, the field emphasized neutrality, at Minnowbrook I, discussions of social equity and neutrality in public administration began to intersect. Hosted by the Maxwell School in 1968, Minnowbrook provided scholars with a space to discuss the role and contributions of public administration (Gooden & Portillo, 2011). Set against the backdrop of a war, political protests, and heightened racial tensions, Minnowbrook was a space for emerging scholars to critique the field's trajectory and evaluate public administration's role in resolving the country's most salient social issues (Wooldridge & Gooden, 2009; Frederickson, 2010). Attending scholars came to a common consensus: the normative premises and practices of analysis guiding the field were inadequate to mitigate the U.S.' social turmoil (La Porte, 1971). In response to these shortcomings, Frederickson proposed that the field of public administration should give more attention to the concept of social equity (Frederickson, 1990; Wooldridge & Gooden, 2009).

Social equity is defined as, "the active commitment to fairness, justice, and equality in the formation of policy, distribution of services, implementation of policy, and management of all institutions serving the public directly or by contract" (Johnson & Svara, 2011, p. 282). As Frederickson (2010) notes, before the 1960s, scholars and practitioners assumed that "good administration of government was equally good for everyone" (p. 75). Recognizing that administrators are not neutral and their actions could result in the unfair implementation of policy, he pushed for scholars and practitioners to emphasize fairness and representation (Frederickson, 2010). From Frederickson's (2005) perspective, pluralistic governments have a tendency to, "systematic-ally discriminate in favor of established, stable bureaucracies and their specialized clientele—and against those minorities who lack political and economic resources" (p. 37). Because of this, administrators must take action that attempts to promote equity in their communities.

The dialogue brought forth at Minnowbrook I led to the develop-ment of New Public Administration (Wooldridge & Gooden, 2009), a movement aimed at adding social equity to the traditional object-ives of efficiency, economy, and effectiveness in public administration (Frederickson, 1980). With time, scholars began to view social equity as the fourth pillar of public administration, along with efficiency, effect-iveness, and economy (Svara & Brunet, 2004, 2005). As social equity research gained traction in the field of public administration, scholars began to give attention to the groups often experiencing inequity: women, people of color, and LGBTQ individuals. In short, we began to give attention to the concept of identity.

Identity in Public Administration

Identity is central to someone's understanding of themselves and their surroundings. Broadly, identity depicts the way individuals can be categorized, as well as group memberships they can attempt to align themselves with (Deaux, 1993). When examining social identity in organ-izational contexts, Ashforth and Mael (1989) define identification as "the perception of oneness with or belongingness to a group, involving direct or vicarious experiences of its successes and failures" (p. 34). Identity for-mation happens through the interaction of how someone perceives them-self and how others perceive them (Headley et al., 2021). This suggests, "that identities and lived experiences are reciprocally related. A person's lived experiences affect his or her history and his or her identity; and those identities influence the person's lived experiences" (Headley et al., 2021, p. 2). Overall, identity is a means to find belongingness in diverse communities; however, it also ties one to the outcomes and perceptions of the social groups they are identified with.

In public administration research, scholars often focus on who has been left out, or othered, in organizations and positions of power. The identities that are often the focus of equity-centered research in public administration (i.e., women, people of color, and LGBTQ individ-uals) are often examined through broader concepts: gender, race, and heteronormativity. Below we consider how each of these categories has been addressed within the field.

Gender and Feminist Theory in Public Administration

When discussions of gender began to gain prominence in the field of public administration, scholars often focused on incorporating the experiences of women (i.e., a feminine perspective) into more traditional discourses of administration. One of the first feminist critiques of public administration, Denhardt and Perkins (1976), argued that theories of organizations so strongly emphasized the experiences of men that scholars were implicitly using the "administrative man" as the basis for all organizational models. Specifically, Denhardt and Perkins (1976) argued that "contemporary theories of organization are largely theories about men in organization, by men, and for men" (p. 379). Eight years later, Ferguson (1984) added an additional feminist critique, suggesting that bureaucracies are inherently gendered with a masculine identity, meaning bureaucracies tend to value qualities and behaviors more commonly associated with men compared to those associated with women. Stivers (1991, 1995) continued to build on this work, providing another discussion that called attention to the exclusion of women in public administration theory. Notably, Stivers (1995) wanted to bring attention to the contributions that women had made in the development of public administration and the administrative state, which had historically been overlooked.

Collectively, these foundational works highlight two central themes. First, the field of public administration has historically excluded women from research and practice. From the genesis of the field to several decades later, men represented the vast majority of the public labor force, as well as scholars of public administration, which was reflected in everything from administrative research to human resource policies. Second, associated with the exclusion of women, the field of public administration had implicitly developed a masculine identity. Meaning even when scholars did not explicitly say that their theories and scholarship centered men, they were often the only identity considered or written about.

Along with focusing on how to include women in public administration, scholars also sought to define gender and understand its application in the public sector. While several definitions of gender have been provided throughout feminist theory, one that is often applied in public administration scholarship is Acker's (2006) definition that describes gender as the "socially constructed differences between men and women and the beliefs and identities that support difference and inequality" (p. 444). From this view, gender is a means to convey power (Scott, 1986), with men and masculinity being prioritized by organizations and institutions. More recent literature uses a broader definition of gender, describing it as a social structure (Humphrey, 2022). Social structures represent human-made restrictions on behavior (Blau, 1977; Bur, 1982). As a social structure, gender creates constraints on how employees can display themselves (Humphrey, 2022). These constraints are established through gendered norms or standards of behavior derived from stereotypes of male and female employees (Mastracci & Bowman, 2015; Mastracci & Arreola, 2016). In sum, gender represents a set of expectations placed on individuals that is derived from sex-based stereo-typical behavior and how each individual chooses to respond to those expectations. Gender is distinct from sex that depicts physical or bio-logical traits of an individual at birth. Regardless, it is important to note that neither of these concepts is fully encompassed by two categories (i.e., men/women for gender or male/female for sex), and instead, we now know that gender exists along a continuum. The continuum is often presented as feminine to masculine, with individuals falling any-where along the continuum or moving fluidly between the binaries at either end.

Another avenue for exploring gender, equity, and feminist theory in public administration has been through legal analysis of gender and sex-based discrimination in the workplace. Sexism is the "endorse-ment of discriminatory or prejudicial beliefs based on sex" (Campbell, Schellenberg, & Senn, 1997, p. 89). With the Civil Rights Act of 1964, sex was listed as a protected category under Title VII, making it unlawful for employers to discriminate against an individual during the employment process due to their sex. It would seem as though this law overlooks gender discrimination. However, legal discussions of sex and gender have evolved through several court rulings that have broadened the legal definition of sex to include gender, one of the first being *Price Waterhouse v Hopkins* (1989). Supporting this broader understanding of sex, the Equal Employment Opportunity Commission states: "sex discrimination involves treating someone (an applicant or employee) unfavorably because of that person's sex, including the person's sexual orientation, gender identity, or pregnancy." This definition highlights how broad the definition of sex has become, and the varying instances which qualify as sex-based discrimination. We discuss the role of law and gender equity in more depth in Chapter 5: The Myth of Legal Remedies.

Overall, the interpretation and application of gender throughout the history of public administration scholarship paints a complex picture. While the initial focus was on incorporating experiences of women, over time, as definitions of sex and gender have broadened, discussions in the field have expanded to explore several concepts related to gender so that research can keep up with the complex lived realities of public administrators and the communities they serve.

Race in Public Administration

While Minnowbrook I took place during the Civil Rights Era when racial tensions in the United States had reached a peak, throughout the field's history we have often seen an avoidance of explicit discussions on race and racism. More than 25 years ago, Alexander (1997) argued that discussions of both race and racism were notably absent from public administration literature. Ten years later, Stivers (2007) described the field's history of addressing race as "mediocre at best" (p. 49). While discussions of race were often incorporated into broader research frames (i.e., representative bureaucracy, diversity management, and cultural competency) over the past several decades, and the killing of George Floyd in the summer of 2020, brought discussions of racial equity to the spotlight within public administration scholarship and practice, there is still limited public administration scholarship in this area.

Similar to gender, race is also a socially constructed concept that many scholars have attempted to define. Race represents "socially defined differences based on physical characteristics, culture, and historical domination and oppression, justified by entrenched beliefs" (Acker, 2006, p. 444). Historically, race has been a means to hierarchically classify individuals (Alexander, 1997), and deeply impacts how an individual experiences their surrounding environment (Carroll, Wright, & Meier, 2019). The hierarchical classification of race prioritizes whiteness (Heckler, 2017). Throughout the history of the United States, there have been debates regarding who is considered "white" (Alexander & Stivers, 2010), which is unsurprising considering the privilege and power associated with identifying as white (Starke et al., 2018).

The hierarchical delineations of race allow for racism. Racism is an ideology that justifies inequity based on race (Ray, 2019). Racism has a systematic quality as patterned discrimination that comes as a result of racism, can generate structural barriers (Stivers, 2007). Recent critiques of race in public administration have emphasized that we should not only be concerned with interpersonal, cultural, or structural racism, but also administrative racism. Administrative racism takes place when the outcomes of public agencies unethically target or injure constituents of color (Starke et al., 2018). Acknowledging both structural racism and administrative racism in public administration presents a difficult task because it requires direct critiques of the institutions that govern us. While there are laws designed to prevent explicit discrimination grounded in racism (e.g., the Civil Rights Act of 1964), overall, we still lack the tools and ability to fully challenge and address racism within our scholarship and practice in public administration.

Recently, public administration scholars have begun to turn their attention to the concept of critical race theory (CRT). CRT was initially developed by legal scholars in the 1970s who felt as though the Civil Rights Movement was coming to an end, and there needed to be additional efforts in understanding the connection between race and the law (Delgado & Stefancic, 1993, 2017). CRT offers "a framework that adopts a race-conscious approach to uncover and better understand institutional and structural racism in our society with the aim of promoting and achieving social justice" (Riccucci, 2021, p. 324). Grounding CRT is the assumption that racism is so deeply entrenched within institutions in the United States that it is systemic (Blessett & Gaynor, 2021). While still within its initial phases of exploration within the field of public administration, CRT has presented a nuanced lens to analyze the implications of race and racism in the public sector.

As Alexander and Stivers (2020) note, "reducing the effects of racism begins with recovering and acknowledging its impact on the historical development of public administration" (p. 1473). Prior to Minnowbrook I, we often did not acknowledge that race had any impact on scholarship or practice within the field of public administration. Following Minnowbrook, which was itself partly inspired by the Civil Rights Era and extreme racial tensions throughout the United States, we have still struggled to fully acknowledge the deep impact race has on public administration. Scholars and practitioners often try to avoid explicit discussions of race, racism, and administrative racism due to race being a "nervous" area of government (Gooden, 2014). As we explore the effects of race in public administration, we regularly rely on other disciplines to aid in our understanding. But, it is imperative that public administration scholars understand that race has shaped our work since the founding of our field and it still impacts the day to day practices within public organizations.

Heteronormativity and Queer Theory in Public Administration

LGBTQ identities are understudied in public administration scholarship (Lee, Learmonth, & Harding, 2008; Larson, 2022). Equity research has primarily focused on race and gender, overlooking the experiences of LGBTQ employees in the public sector (Larson, 2022). With LGBTQ identities located on the margins of public administration research, concepts commonly found in other disciplines (e.g., sociology and psychology) have remained unexamined in scholarship focused on the public sector. Although heteronormativity and queer theory were both coined in 1991 by Michael Warner and Teresa de Lauretis, respectively, these concepts are still relatively new to the field of public administration due to their lack of use in research.

Heteronormativity is defined as an "enduring hierarchical social system that identifies heterosexuality as the standard sexuality and normalizes gender-specific behaviors and roles for men, women, and transgender and non-binary individuals" (Holmes, 2019, p. 1). Within the context of public administration, heteronormativity represents implicit and explicit standards placed on employees to align themselves with the prevailing ethos of the organization (Lee et al., 2008). Deconstructing heteronormativity is often a central focus of queer theory, which is a "poststructuralist tool that deconstructs assumptions of normality" (Larson, 2022, p. 8). Theorists in these research areas have often sought to challenge heteronormativity (Rumens, De Souza, & Brewis, 2019), while highlighting the experiences of those perceived as failing to align with heteronormative expectations of behavior.

Discriminatory behavior against individuals that identify as LGBTQ is often described through the terms transphobia and homophobia. Transphobic behavior is depicted by, "an emotional disgust toward individuals who do not conform to society's gender expectations" (Hill & Willoughby, 2005, p. 533). While this definition focuses on the emotional response someone has, it is important to note that this emotional response can turn into actions or behaviors that attempt to target someone based on their gender identity. Similarly, homophobia describes "a wide range of negative emotions, attitudes, and behaviors toward homosexual people" (Haaga, 1991, p. 171). In short, the distinction between transphobia and homophobia often stems from whether someone is being discriminated against due to their gender identity or sexual orientation.

Public administration scholars exploring LGBTQ identities have studied this topic from a variety of angles. One means that scholars have used to study LGBTQ identities in the public sector is by analyzing legal protections (Riccucci & Gossett, 1996; Lewis, 1997; Colvin, 2020). This area of research explores specific court cases and laws to highlight the evolution of LGBTQ protections in the United States. Others have sought to understand LGBTQ employee perspectives. These studies have found that highlighting the workplace satisfaction of LGBTQ federal employees tends to lag that of other federal employees (Lewis & Pitts, 2017; Federman & Elias, 2017), and that LGBTQ employees report higher levels of turnover intention (Sabharwal et al., 2019). Finally, some scholars have sought to identify how to improve organizational policies focused on supporting transgender and nonbinary employees, highlighting, in particular, the importance of updating human resource policies to support the experiences of LGBTQ organizational members (Elias, 2017; Elias & Colvin, 2019). While there have been great strides in LGBTQ scholarship in the field of public administration, research in this area continues to be underrepresented in comparison to other identities, such as race and gender.

With the current lack of research on heteronormativity and queer theory in public administration, these are opportune areas for analysis. By including heteronormativity as an area of focus in this work, we hope to provide a more comprehensive understanding of identity in the public sector workforce that extends beyond discussions of race and gender. Even though race, gender, and heteronormativity are not all encompassing of the identities present among employees working in public organizations, or among the constituents that public organizations serve, collectively, they provide a broad lens to explore identity in the public sector.

Accounting for Multiple Identities

While studying identities in isolation can provide valuable information on the public sector workforce, several scholars have focused on studying the intersection of multiple identities to provide a deeper understanding of employee experiences. The most common framework used to study multiple interacting identities in the field of public administration is intersectionality. However, we present historically grounded positionality as an additional frame to supplement the field's understanding of intersectionality and provide another avenue to explore the relationship between multiple identities in the public sector.

Intersectionality in Public Administration

Intersectionality was first coined by Kimberlé Crenshaw in 1989. Crenshaw (1989) used intersectionality as a legal framework to explore how women of color, specifically Black women, are oppressed in the U.S. legal system by analyzing three notable court cases: *DeGraffenreid v. General Motors*, *Moore v. Hughes Helicopters*, and *Payne v. Travenol*. Through her analysis of these cases, Crenshaw (1989) shows the complexity of intersecting identities and the compounding disadvantage experienced by those holding multiple marginalized identities.

Among these three cases, *DeGraffenreid v. General Motors* provides a helpful example that highlights the complexity of identity in the workplace, as well as the inability of public institutions to address discrimination of historically marginalized identities. Before 1964, General Motors did not employ any Black women (Crenshaw, 1989). Between 1964 and 1970, General Motors only employed one Black woman that worked as a janitor. By 1973, the company employed 155 Black women. However, in response to a recession in 1974, the company fired several employees using a last hired-first fired policy that resulted in every Black woman hired after 1970 being fired from the General Motors Saint Louis branch. In 1975, Emma DeGraffenreid, along with other Black woman who had also lost their jobs, filed a discrimination claim against General Motors. The plaintiffs argued that "the 'last hired-first fired' lay off policies of the defendants discriminated against them as Black women, and are therefore a perpetuation of past discriminatory practices" (*DeGraffenreid v. General Motors*, 1976). However, the court argued that the plaintiffs,

> Should not be allowed to combine statutory remedies to create a new "super-remedy" which would give them relief beyond what the drafters of the relevant statutes intended. Thus, this lawsuit must be examined to see if it states a cause of action for race discrimination, sex discrimination, or alternatively either, but not a combination of both.
>
> (*DeGraffenreid v. General Motors*, 1976)

The Court ultimately said that the Black women in this case could either sue based on their race *or* their sex, as each were protected categories, but the combination of the two was not protected. What the Court was unable to see in this situation was how intersecting identities have the ability to create unique forms of oppression and discrimination. The discrimination faced by this group was not solely grounded in their identity as women, or their identity as Black, but the intersection of their identities as Black women (Crenshaw, 1989). This framework and understanding of oppression helped open new doors in how discrimination of marginalized identities could be studied.

During the 1990s and 2000s, intersectionality gained popularity across several academic disciplines, leading scholars to generate broader definitions of the concept. For example, Bearfield (2009) defines intersectionality as, "an interdisciplinary theoretical framework that is focused on the intersection identity categories" (p. 384). This broadens the definition of intersectionality from more narrowly focusing on the experiences of Black women, to attempting to recognize the various identities present within the public sector.

Within the context of public administration research, scholars have explored intersectionality in relation to leadership (Nelson & Piatak, 2021), representative bureaucracy (Fay, Hicklin Fryar, Meier, & Wilkins, 2020), reporting of sex-based discrimination (Yu, 2021), and other topics. Nelson and Piatak (2021) highlight the complexity of intersectionality, finding that women of color perceive higher levels of cooperation among their work unit and feelings of empowerment, while also perceiving "lower levels of fairness, openness, and support" (p. 310). Fay et al. (2020) explore intersectionality in representation within U.S. colleges and universities, finding that "the intersectional match-up (faculty sex-race/ethnicity combinations being the same as student sex-race/ethnicity combinations) provided the greatest policy outcome gains" (p. 348), for Black men and Latinx students. However, they did not find improved outcomes for Black women. Yu (2021) adds an additional layer to this discussion in her study on the reporting behavior of sex-based discrimination from women in federal law enforcement when they have experienced sex-based discrimination. Contrary to her hypotheses, Yu (2021) found that women of color are actually more likely to report sex-based discrimination than white women. Collectively, these studies highlight the importance of accounting for the multiple identities someone holds, as their findings indicate that scholars and practitioners can gain additional understanding from studying at these intersections.

Intersectionality research has been essential to improving the field's understanding of diversity and equity. By examining the interaction of multiple identities, we gain a deeper understanding of the reality that public servants face when navigating their organizations. However, there is still an opportunity to know more. While intersectionality provides an improvement from focusing on a single identity, it still lacks a discussion of contextual or environmental factors that influence how someone experiences their identity. Historically grounded positionality provides an opportunity to address this shortcoming.

Historically Grounded Positionality as a New Framework

Historically grounded positionality is a framework for understanding how the past shapes the present, and the current position from which we view the world and choose to display ourselves. In the context of positionality, identity is both situational and fluid, meaning we should anticipate that a person's identity can vary depending on their environment (Doan & Portillo, 2017). Anthias (2008) states: "Identity involves individual and collective narratives of self and other, presentation and labeling, myths of origin and myths of destiny with associated strategies and identifications" (p. 8). As described in the definition from Anthias (2008), identity is not only about the self, but also about the other. How other people perceive you may be just as important as how you understand your own identity when it comes to how you are treated. Positionality attempts to account for the other people and factors inherently present within organizations and environments when managing one's own identity.

This approach derives from a foundation of feminist positionality scholarship and integrates intersectionality, while also recognizing how geographic and temporal nuances influence individual and community understandings of identity (Doan & Portillo, 2017). Where and when someone is experiencing their identity are important contextual factors that shape how identity is understood by the individual and cultures. Understandings of identity have been evolving for centuries, shaped by both the individual and their surrounding environment. Ultimately, we suggest historically grounded positionality is another framework to understand identity within public sector organizations. By relying on this framework, our purpose is to highlight that identity is positional – dependent on the institutions, time period, and communities an individual engages with.

Conclusion

As a field, our understanding of identity has become more nuanced. There are now frameworks to understand the role of gender, race, and sexual orientation that have made it into our theoretical and empirical scholarship. Many scholars have taken this a step further and considered intersectionality, noting how multiple identities interact to create unique experiences for individuals within organizations and communities. This scholarship has shaped the way that practitioners understand and practice public administration. However, many of our current approaches to understanding identity in public administration fail to take into account historical context. Historically grounded positionality builds on feminist and intersectional traditions to present a framework that takes into account the ways that identities continues to evolve. Before turning back to a more nuanced discussion of the historically grounded positionality framework, we present some of the foundational myths of our field and how they obscured the role of identity in public administration.

In the next chapter, we build on this discussion of identity and explore the myth of merit. We suggest that, over time, definitions of merit have changed and evolved. Specifically, public organizations and institutions have changed the meaning of merit, so that it can apply to those deemed deserving and work against those considered undeserving. However, expectations of who is and is not deserving have often been grounded in identity, rather than skill set or professional knowledge. The myth of merit continues to shape how we discuss identity in our field, even though the foundations of the myth have been consistently questioned.

Works Cited

Cases

DeGraffenreid v. GENERAL MOTORS ASSEMBLY DIV., ETC., 413 F. Supp. 142 (E.D. Mo. 1976).

Literature

Acker, J. (2006). Inequality regimes: Gender, class, and race in organizations. *Gender & Society, 20*(4), 441–464.

Alexander, J. (1997). Avoiding the issue: Racism and administrative responsibility in public administration. *American Review of Public Administration, 27*(4), 343–361.

Alexander, J., & Stivers, C. (2010). An ethic of race for public administration. *Administrative Theory & Praxis, 32*(4), 578–597.

———. (2020). Racial bias: A buried cornerstone of the Administrative State. *Administration & Society, 52*(10), 1470–1490.

Anthias, F. (2008). Thinking through the lens of translocational positionality: An intersectionality frame for understanding identity and belonging. *Translocations: Migration and Social Change, 4*(1), 5–20.

Ashforth, B. E., & Mael, F. (1989). Social identity theory and the organization. *Academy of Management Review, 14*(1), 20–39.

Bearfield, D. A. (2009). Equity at the intersection: Public administration and the study of gender. *Public Administration Review, 69*(3), 383–386.

Benton, M. (2018). "Just the way things are around here": Racial segregation, critical junctures, and path dependence in Saint Louis. *Journal of Urban History, 44*(6), 1113–1130.

Blau, P. M. (1977). *Inequality and heterogeneity: A primitive theory of social structure.* Free Press.

Blessett, B., & Gaynor, T. S. (2021). Race, racism and administrative callousness: Using critical race theory for a race-conscious public administration. *Public Integrity, 23*(5), 455–458.

Burt, R. S. (1982). *Toward a structural theory of action: Network models of social structure, perception, and action.* Academic Press.

Campbell, B., Schellenberg, E. G., & Senn, C. Y. (1997). Evaluating measures of contemporary sexism. *Psychology of Women Quarterly, 21*(1), 89–102.

Carroll, K., Wright, K., & Meier, K. J. (2019). Minority public administrators: Managing organizational demands while acting as an advocate. *The American Review of Public Administration, 49*(7), 810–824.

Colvin, R. (2020). Special issue on gender identity and expression and sexual orientation (LGBTQ+) in the public and nonprofit contexts. *Administrative Theory & Praxis, 42*(2), 111–114.

Crenshaw, K. (1989). Demarginalizing the intersection of race and sex: A black feminist critique of antidiscrimination doctrine, feminist theory and anti-racist politics. *University of Chicago Legal Forum*, 139–168.

Deaux, K. (1993). Reconstructing social identity. *Personality and Social Psychology Bulletin, 19*(1), 4–12.

Delgado, R., & Stefancic, J. (1993). Critical race theory: An annotated bibliography. *Virginia Law Review, 79*(2), 461–516.

———. (2017). *Critical race theory: An introduction* (Vol. 20). New York University Press.

Denhardt, R. B., & Perkins, J. (1976). The coming of death of administrative man. *Public Administration Review, 36*(4), 379–384.

Doan, A. E., & Portillo, S. (2017). Not a woman, but a soldier: Exploring identity through translocational positionality. *Sex Roles, 76*(3–4), 236–249.

Donohue Jr, R. H. (2020). Shades of blue: A review of the hiring, recruitment, and selection of female and minority police officers. *Social Science Journal, 58*(4), 1–15.

Elias, N. M. (2017). Constructing and implementing transgender policy for public administration. *Administration & Society, 49*(1), 20–47.

Elias, N., & Colvin, R. (2020). A third option: Understanding and assessing non-binary gender policies in the United States. *Administrative Theory & Praxis, 42*(2), 191–211.

Fay, D. L., Hicklin Fryar, A., Meier, K. J., & Wilkins, V. (2020). Intersectionality and equity: Dynamic bureaucratic representation in higher education. *Public Administration, 99*(2), 335–352.

Federman, P. S., & Elias, N. M. (2017). Beyond the lavender scare: LGBT and heterosexual employees in the federal workplace. *Public Integrity, 19*(1), 22–40.

Ferguson, K. (1984). *The feminist case against bureaucracy*. Temple University Press.

Frederickson, H. G. (1980). *New public administration*. University Alabama Press.

———. (1990). Public administration and social equity. *Public Administrative Review, 50*(2), 228–237.

———. (2005). The state of social equity in American public administration. *National Civic Review, 94*, 31–38.

———. (2010). *Social equity and public administration: Origins, developments, and applications*. Sharpe.

Funk, K. (2019). If the shoe fits: Gender role congruity and evaluations of public managers. *Journal of Behavioral Public Administration, 2*(1). https://doi.org/10.30636/jbpa.21.48

Gooden, S. (2014). *Race and social equity: A nervous area of government.* Sharpe.

Gooden, S., & Portillo, S. (2011). Advancing social equity in the Minnowbrook tradition. *Journal of Public Administration Research and Theory, 21*(11), i61–i76.

Haaga, D. A. (1991). Homophobia? *Journal of Social Behavior and Personality, 6*(1), 171.

Headley, A. M., Wright, J. E., & Meier, K. J. (2021). Bureaucracy, democracy, and race: The limits of symbolic representation. *Public Administration Review, 81*(6), 1033–1043.

Heckler, N. (2017). Publicly desired color-blindness: Whiteness as a realized public value. *Administrative Theory & Praxis, 39*(3), 175–192.

Hill, D. B., & Willoughby, B. L. (2005). The development and validation of the genderism and transphobia scale. *Sex Roles, 53*(7), 531–544.

Holmes IV, O. (2019). The antecedents and outcomes of heteronormativity in organizations. In *Oxford research encyclopedia of business and management.* Oxford University Press.

House-Niamke, S., & Eckerd, A. (2021). Institutional injustice: How public administration has fostered and can ameliorate racial disparities. *Administration & Society, 53*(2), 305–324.

Humphrey, N. (2022). Gender and public service motivation: Recognizing gender as a social structure. In P. Shields & N. Elias (Eds.), *Handbook on gender and public administration.* Edward Elgar Publishing.

Johnson, N., & Svara, J. (2011). *Justice for all: Promoting social equity in public administration.* Sharpe.

La Porte, T. (1971). The recovery of relevance in the study of public organization. In F. Marini (Ed.), *Toward a new public administration: The Minnowbrook perspective.* Chandler Publishing Company.

Larson, S. J. (2022). Actions for queering American public administration. *Administration & Society, 54*(1), 145–163.

Lee, H., Learmonth, M., & Harding, N. (2008). Queer(y)ing public administration. *Public Administration, 86*(1), 149–167.

Lewis, G. B. (1997). Lifting the ban on gays in the civil service: Federal policy toward gay and lesbian employees since the Cold War. *Public Administration Review, 57*(5), 387–395.

Lewis, G. B., & Pitts, D. W. (2017). LGBT—Heterosexual differences in perceptions of fair treatment in the federal service. *American Review of Public Administration, 47*(5), 574–587.

Lippmann, R. (2020, June 11). Barton acknowledges racial divide in St. Louis county police department. *Saint Louis Public Radio.* https://news.stlpublicra dio.org/politics-issues/2020-06-11/barton-acknowledges-racial-divide-in-st-louis-county-police-department.

Mastracci, S., & Arreola, V. I. (2016). Gendered organizations: How human resource management practices produce and reproduce administrative man. *Administrative Theory & Praxis, 38*(2), 137–149.

Mastracci, S., & Bowman, L. (2015). Public agencies, gendered organizations: The future of gender studies in public management. *Public Management Review, 17*(6), 857–875.

Nelson, A., & Piatak, J. (2021). Intersectionality, leadership, and inclusion: How do racially underrepresented women fare in the federal government? *Review of Public Personnel Administration, 41*(2), 294–318.

Ray, V. (2019). A theory of racialized organizations. *American Sociological Review, 84*(1), 26–53.

Riccucci, N. M. (2021). Applying critical race theory to public administration scholarship. *Perspectives on Public Management and Governance, 4*(4), 324–338.

Riccucci, N. M., & Gossett, C. W. (1996). Employment discrimination in state and local government: The lesbian and gay male experience. *American Review of Public Administration, 26*(2), 175–200.

Rumens, N., De Souza, E. M., & Brewis, J. (2019). Queering queer theory in management and organization studies: Notes toward queering heterosexuality. *Organization Studies, 40*(4), 593–612.

Sabharwal, M., Levine, H., D'Agostino, M., & Nguyen, T. (2019). Inclusive work practices: Turnover intentions among LGBT employees of the US federal government. *American Review of Public Administration, 49*(4), 482–494.

Scott, J. W. (1986). Gender: A useful category of historical analysis. *American Historical Review, 91*(5), 1053–1075.

Sklansky, D. A. (2005). Not your father's police department: Making sense of the new demographics of law enforcement. *Journal of Criminal Law & Criminology, 96*(3), 1209–1244.

Smith, A. E., Hassan, S., Hatmaker, D., DeHart-Davis, L., & Humphrey, N. M. (2020). Gender, race, and experiences of workplace incivility in public organizations. *Review of Public Personnel Administration, 41*(4), 674–699.

Starke, A. M., Heckler, N., & Mackey, J. (2018). Administrative racism: Public administration education and race. *Journal of Public Affairs Education, 24*(4), 469–489.

Stivers, C. (1991). Toward a feminist perspective in public administration theory. *Women & Politics, 10*(4), 49–65.

———. (1995). Settlement women and bureau men: Constructing a usable past for public administration. *Public Administration Review, 55*(6), 522–529.

———. (2007). "So poor and so black": Hurricane Katrina, public administration, and the issue of race. *Public Administration Review, 67*, 48–56.

Svara, J. H., & Brunet, J. R. (2004). Filling in the skeletal pillar: Addressing social equity in introductory courses in public administration. *Journal of Public Affairs Education, 10*(2), 99–109.

———. (2005). Social equity is a pillar of public administration. *Journal of Public Affairs Education, 11*(3), 253–258.

Taylor, A. N. (2013). Segregation, education, and blurring the lines of division in St. Louis. *Saint Louis University Public Law Review, 33*(1), 183.

Treisman, R. (2019, October 30). Missouri cop who says he was told "Tone down your gayness" wins discrimination case. *NPR*. www.npr.org/2019/10/30/774805535/missouri-cop-who-says-he-was-told-tone-down-your-gayness-wins-discrimination-cas.

Van Oot, T., & Van Berkel, J. (2020, May 30). "Change can't come fast enough": Minnesota, U.S. leaders respond to arrest in George Floyd's death. *Star Tribune*. www.startribune.com/change-can-t-come-fast-enough-minnesota-u-s-leaders-respond-to-arrest-in-george-floyd-s-death/570869811/

Wooldridge, B., & Gooden, S. (2009). The epic of social equity: Evolution, essence, and emergence. *Administrative Theory & Praxis, 31*(2), 222–234.

Yu, H. H. (2021). Intersectionality and non-reporting behavior: Perceptions from women of color in federal law enforcement. *Review of Public Personnel Administration*. https://doi.org/10.1177/0734371X211006189

3   The Myth of Merit

On March 14, 2014, the New York Times Editorial Board ran a column with the headline "A Fire Department for the 21st Century." The editorial addressed the settlement of a lawsuit in which the city paid close to 100 million dollars to Black and Latinx residents who were denied the chance to work for the city's fire department. The lawsuit, brought in 2007, charged that the entrance examination to join the department was racially biased (Santora & Schwirtz, 2014). This was not the first time the city was charged with bias in its hiring and promotion practices.

In her examination of the history of discrimination in the New York City Fire Department (FDNY), Marcus and Otis (2015) described a confrontation in 2012 between Captain Paul Washington, the leader of the Vulcans society, a fraternal organization created in 1940 to address the needs of Black firefighters in New York City, and Deputy Chief Paul Mannix, the founder of Merit Matters. While the confrontation on that night occurred at a tutorial event, organized by the Vulcans for Black people interested in joining the fire department, the true source of conflict was the 2007 lawsuit. According to Otis, the Vulcans argued that the examination did not accurately predict who would perform well on the job and that it discriminated against prospective firefighters of color. However, members of Merit Matters, an organization created in an attempt to preserve traditional examination-based hiring practices of the FDNY, opposed the lawsuit. While there is a large literature detailing the discriminatory history of examinations, and questions concerning the validity of those examinations (Portillo et al., 2020), it should not be surprising that organizations like Merit Matters continue to defend what many consider *traditional merit*. On the surface, the conflict between the two men could be framed as individuals who have taken opposing sides in the city's legal dispute, but at its core, this conflict reflects a long historic problem in American public administration – what do we mean by merit?

DOI: 10.4324/9781003322795-3

New York City is not alone in the struggle to define merit. Redding, California is a town of just under 100,000 people, located in the northern part of the state. There is an entire section dedicated to commendations and awards in the policy manual for the town's Police Department. The section lists all of the awards an individual could earn and provides a definition for each. In Redding, there are 12 different awards. Interestingly, there is both an award for meritorious conduct and another called the Merit Award. The meritorious conduct award is "Awarded to any employee for meritorious service or excellent performance in an assignment of great responsibility where the officer distinguishes himself/herself of the Police Department while carrying out the assignment" (Redding Police Department, 2019). However, the Merit Award is

> Awarded to any Redding Police Department employee or volunteer for outstanding performance of duties under unusual, complicated or hazardous conditions. This award may also be given to any Redding Police Department employee or volunteer for the outstanding or superior performance of any assignment over a prolonged period of time.
>
> (Redding Police Department, 2019, p. 5)

Winners are announced after a review of the nominations by the Meritorious Conduct Board.

While both awards intend to reward outstanding service, the specific definition of merit or meritorious (deserving of merit) seems to shift depending on the circumstances. In this, the department is not particularly unique. Is merit the acknowledgment of a particularly heroic act? Is it a way to recognize someone who has performed well over a sustained period? Or maybe both? The truth is merit is one of those concepts that we believe we understand until we must give a specific definition. It is only then that we realize that we aren't always describing the same thing.

Looking beyond awards, in American public administration, the word merit is commonly associated with the crowning achievement of the Progressive Era – the civil service system – otherwise known as the merit system. The merit system was created to replace patronage-based hiring practices with one that would allow us to select the best person for the job. Yet, we still are not exactly clear with what we mean when we use the word merit. Krislov (1964) notes,

> Perhaps the most remarkable aspect of the American attitudes toward merit in employment has been their naiveté and simplicity

of approach. The significant fact is that 'the dog did not bark in the night.' Little examination of the problems in selection and promotion of the 'Most qualified' is to be found in the scholarly literature. (p. 65)

Ultimately our field has done little to define this central concept.

In this chapter, we point out that despite a long history of merit based examinations in American public administration, the actual definition of merit has always been quite murky. In the traditional reading, shortly after the passage of the Pendleton Act two concepts of merit emerged. One focused on individual competence and performance, and another based on the ability of the hiring manager to determine who might be a good fit for their organization. We propose a different reading of the field's history – merit as deservedness. Building on the discussion of identity from the previous chapter, we use the concept of social construction to demonstrate how the battle of merit represents a century-long fight to determine who deserves to be a public servant. While the idea of merit as deservedness is not inherently controversial, much like in the example of the FDNY, we believe that the battles have often been fought along racial, ethnic, and gender lines. Yet, this fight has not been exclusively about race, ethnicity, and gender. Toward the end of the chapter, we expand this argument even further to illustrate the long, and troubling, history of Lesbian, Gay, Bisexual, Transgender, Queer, and other sexual and gender minority (LGBTQ) public servants and their fight to be recognized as deserving of public employment.

Merit and the Protestant Work Ethic

Mosher (1982) ties the definition of merit to roots in the Protestant work ethic. He points to two definitions of merit that he describes as "dominantly ethical" (p. 218). The first is that employers should reward people for their hard work (past performance) or demonstration of their potential (performance on their written examinations). This view is similar to Van Riper's (1958) position and the language used by the Senate Committee on Civil Service and Retrenchment in discussion on the Pendleton Act. Borrowing from the British civil service system, the Pendleton Act relied on competitive examinations, some degree of job security or tenure, and the notion of neutrality (Van Riper, 1958, p. 98).

The second is that merit establishes a basis for making a judgment or consideration. Mosher (1982) notes, "A judge considers an argument on its merits; a scientist considers a proposition or argument on its merits; an employing officer considers a prospective employee on his or her merit" (p. 218). In other words, in this definition merit is more subjective. It isn't rooted in one's performance on an exam, or a scientific evaluation of one's past experience. But, instead, it is based on the judgment of the hiring manager based on an individual's potential value to the organization.

As people slide back and forth between the two definitions, one strictly focused on past or potential performance, and the other based on much more subjective criteria, the idea of objectivity moves from a solid principle into an idea that is much harder to pin down. Toward the end of *Democracy and the Public Service*, Mosher (1982) appears to recognize this more fully and pushes back on the position taken by merit system purists. He notes,

> …obviously merit has always had a lot of other considerations to compete with. It has never been pure in practice, or even in law. And maybe it should not be, even if we had the knowledge and skill to make it pure.
>
> (p. 219)

Whereas Mosher places these deviations from pure merit in one category, it is essential to see them in a broader context. Schnieder and Ingram (1993) note that policymakers often resort to socially constructed images of groups and populations to determine who is worthy of rewards and benefits. In the hands of skilled, or powerful, actors, populations can be constructed as positive or negative, deviant or heroic, deserving or undeserving. For example, following the tough financial times faced by the United States during the 1970s, there was a strong desire to reform many government policies. This was especially true of welfare policy that, depending on who was asked, was seen as either essential aid to families in need or wasteful spending that trapped families in a generational cycle of poverty.

In an attempt to illustrate alleged fraud and abuse of the federal welfare system, conservative politicians constructed an archetype to shift the political debate – the welfare queen. Based on the story of a woman from Chicago who was alleged to have defrauded multiple social welfare programs out of 150,000 dollars, the term welfare queen was used by conservative politicians to argue that the system needed to be reformed. While the race of the original woman was not widely known, it was clear that many Americans *knew* exactly which racial group she belonged to. As race and culture critic Gene Demby (2013) noted, "In the popular imagination, the stereotype of the 'welfare queen' is thoroughly raced— she's an indolent black woman, living off the largesse of taxpayers."

Throughout the 1980s and 1990s, politicians, media figures, and others used the concept of the welfare queen to trade on some of the hateful and enduring stereotypes of Black, poor, single mothers. It is argued that socially constructed public identity of the welfare queen was one of the driving forces behind a sweeping welfare reform passed in the mid-1990s (Hancock, 2004). While this racialized archetype was used to push for welfare reform, the vast majority of welfare recipients at the time (and to this day) do not fit that stereotype. In fact, the majority of welfare recipients in the United States are white (Gilliom, 2001). While we generally think of this type of social construction in terms of legislative policy, Schnieder and Ingram (1993) note that all three bodies – executive, legislative, and judicial – have used this framing to advance their political agendas.

It is important to note that the social construction of populations can also result in framing that is more positive, and as a result that specific population is seen as more deserving of public resources, aid, and/or sympathy. For instance, during the period of financial hardship that resulted in the creation of the welfare queen trope, the contrast to a different population group, farmers, could not have been starker. Because of high interest rates, high levels of borrowing and overproduction, many farms were pushed into bankruptcy because of their inability to pay off their loans (Barnett, 2000). Because several of the farms were owned by families, the term family farm emerged as a way to describe those most impacted by the crisis. Unlike the welfare queen, the image invoked by the term family farmer was that of a white, hardworking family who, through no fault of their own, had fallen on bad times. As the crisis grew, politicians, musicians, and many in the media used the term as a way of generating sympathy for the farmers. The positive framing of the socially constructed family farmer helped produce one of the biggest agricultural reform efforts in American history. Significant financial resources flowed to farmers through legislation at the same time that support to families was severely restricted via welfare reform.

In terms of the merit system, throughout our history, we have constructed narratives of deserving and undeserving populations to decide who should work in the public sector. In each example, a case is made for why and when it is ok to set aside our traditional views of merit to make an exception for a particular group. While people tend to view preferences for veterans favorably, women, racial and ethnic minorities, and other marginalized populations are often seen as undeserving of their positions. And, even when they are not explicitly considered undeserving, they are often seen and treated as less deserving than white men.

In the next section, we will discuss the adoption and spread of the merit ideal. We will also show that at various times, organizations have set aside their belief in merit principles to reward groups who they deem are more deserving. Instead of viewing this practice as an exception, or necessary flexibility, we argue that it is a common and accepted practice.

Merit as Deservedness: Who Deserves to be a Public Servant

When people discuss the idea of merit in American public administration, it is taken for granted that it is a way of conveying that institutions should hire the best person for the job. As Van Riper (1958) noted, this idea was cemented in the language used by the Senate Committee on Civil Service and Retrenchment discussion on the Pendleton Act (p. 98). Borrowing from the British, the Pendleton Act relied on competitive examinations, some degree of job security or tenure, and the notion of neutrality.

However, we did not simply transfer the British system and replant it on American soil. An exciting development in the American use of examinations was the desire for a practical element. As Van Riper (1958) would say, they could not be strictly theoretical but had to be related to the duties being performed (p. 99). One should also note that discretion has always been built into the merit selection process because of the separation of powers in the U.S. system. The Pendleton Act laid out the civil service merit system by the legislature, but the power of appointment resides with the executive. The merit system acts as a guide in decision-making by the executive branch. Ideas such as the rule of three, which would allow the hiring officer to select from among the top three candidates, but not necessarily the top candidate, and other methods, provide the executive with a bit of discretionary power when making hiring or promotion decisions (Van Riper, 1958). This discretionary power, intentionally or not, created space for those in charge of overseeing the merit system to divide populations into those who deserve public employment and those who do not.

What Whites Deserve: Segregation and the Federal Service

One common understanding of the word merit is rooted in the concept of deservingness (Anderson, 2013). In colloquial terms, when we say that an idea merits further investigation, it is a suggestion that the idea has value and is worthy of greater attention or study. Conversely, when an issue does not merit our attention, we implicitly stigmatize it with the suggestion that it is of lesser value. This understanding of merit as deservedness isn't limited to things that grab our intellectual curiosity. Historically, in our public personnel systems, we have used the idea of merit as deservedness to advance the career of some segments of the population and to thwart the advancement of others.

Perhaps there is no greater example of this than the introduction of segregation of Black workers in federal employment. For much of the twentieth century, Black federal workers were essentially walled off, or segregated from their white contemporaries. In practice, this meant that in most jobs, Black employees were not permitted to work alongside white employees. However, segregation was not limited to the actual workspace. This included the lunchroom, bathrooms, and sometimes entire buildings.

In the movie *Hidden Figures*, there is a scene where Katherine Johnson, a Black human computer, played by Taraji P. Henson goes to use the restroom. When she is asked why she was away from her desk for 40 minutes she explains that she has to travel half a mile across Langley Air Force base, on foot, while wearing stockings and heels, to use the bathroom because there are no restrooms for African Americans on the side of campus where she has been temporarily assigned to assist on the NASA space mission. The fact that she did not have a bathroom on that side of campus did not merit consideration by managers in the organization, who were all white and had ready access to restrooms throughout the campus. In the movie her white male boss dramatically removes the sign saying whites only on the restroom in their building. In reality, bathrooms remained segregated at Langley Air Force base until the entire federal system was forced to desegregate accommodations.

However, the federal workforce was not always segregated as a matter of policy. Prior to the election of President Woodrow Wilson, it was not uncommon to find federal workers of all races working together. However, shortly after his election, several of his southern cabinet members called for the races to be separated. Upon noticing white and Black women working together, the Acting Treasury Secretary remarked in a memo "I feel sure that this must go against the grain of the white women and suggested that only white women should work in close proximity of other white women" (King, 1995, p. 3). Others objected to the idea of white employees reporting to Black supervisors, indicating that it upset the "cleanliness" of the social order (King, 2007). These objections were not tied to any indicators of performance or lack of qualifications, although it was not uncommon for many white people to believe that Black people were inherently inferior just by nature of being Black. No, the objection in this case was the belief that white employees deserved better.

Segregation of the federal workforce flourished under President Wilson, despite protest from W. E. B. Du Bois, the acclaimed scholar and activist and a founder of the NAACP. In 1913, in both a public "Open Letter" and in private correspondence, Du Bois chastised President Wilson's silence on segregation in the federal civil service and the dismissal of Black public officials. This was quite an about face, since just a year before Du Bois had endorsed Wilson for the presidency with the belief that he would be fair toward Black people. While initially there was debate about how much Wilson knew about the practice, his private papers confirm that not only did he know about the segregation of federal workers, but he supported it, arguing that he believed that segregation would reduce friction between the races (King, 1995). Despite evidence that the policy actively hurt the social and professional prospects of Black workers, by siding with the segregationists, President Wilson prioritized the comfort of white employees and cabinet members. By the end of the Wilson administration, segregation as an administrative practice was firmly entrenched into the federal service.

The 1940s and 1950s: Redefining Merit as a Means of Exclusion

African Americans were not the only group to undergo this negative social construction. During the 1940s and 1950s, there was a period of clear and persistent discrimination against the LGBTQ community by the U.S. government. Referred to as the Lavender Scare, this era saw the systematic removal of gay employees (or suspected gay employees) from their positions in the federal government because governmental leaders claimed they were more susceptible to blackmail and thus a security risk (Elias, 2017; Federman & Rishel Elias, 2017). The Lavender Scare provides an opportunity to explore how merit is a concept that has been adapted throughout history as a means to define who is a *good* employee, with potentially harmful implications for marginalized groups – in this instance the LGBTQ community.

We see some of the first actions of the Lavender Scare in 1947, when a list of self-confessed and alleged "homosexuals" was sent to the State Department for investigation by Senate appropriations subcommittee (Lewis, 1997). Two years later, the Hoey Committee was formed in Congress to specifically review the employment of suspected queer federal employees (Lewis, 1997), marking the federal government's next significant action to systematically removing LGBTQ employees from their positions. Treatment of gay, lesbian, and queer employees only worsened over the next few years – definitions of a "good employee" begin to change to specifically include heterosexuality, and with those changes, LGBTQ employees were no longer protected by the standards of the Pendleton Act of 1883.

Altering the Expectations of Merit

In 1953, President Eisenhower signed Executive Order 10450 that listed sexual perversion as a potential threat to national security and allowed the government to justifiably dismiss gay, lesbian, and queer employees (Lewis, 1997). In the years following, hundreds of employees would be removed from their positions with the federal government (Lewis, 1997). As discussed in the previous chapter, the Pendleton Act of 1883 helped formally establish the civil service merit system through three core standards (Ingraham, 2006; Woodard, 2005). With the signing of Executive Order 10450, we see alterations in the second core standard of The Pendleton Act. This standard, "prohibited firing federal employees for any reason other than cause" (Ingraham, 2006, p. 486). Executive Order 10450 from President Eisenhower provided cause – specifically saying that someone's sexual orientation could be cause for firing. While there are several legal actions in the decades that followed these events attempting to protect LGBTQ employees from discrimination (see Table 3.1), actions from the 1940s to the 1960s clearly highlight a desire to rewrite the definition of merit in a way that penalizes LGBTQ employees, protecting the heteronormativity of the bureaucracy.

Not long after the signing of Executive Order 10450, the courts began to provide parameters for what causes would justify the dismissal of gay, lesbian, and queer employees. Notably, in *Scott vs Macy*, the Circuit Court of the District of Columbia ruled that firing an employee for "immoral conduct" was not adequate justification, and the agency must explain how the conduct impacted job competence (1965). In short, public agencies cannot dismiss someone simply because of their sexual orientation – their conduct must relate to their work performance. However, in 1966, the Chairman of the Civil Service Commission, John Macy Jr. argued, "Person[s] about whom there is evidence that they have engaged in or solicited others to engage in homosexual or sexually perverted acts with them, without evidence of rehabilitation, are not suitable for Federal employment." Furthermore, the Chairman argued, "the revulsion of other employees" and "the offense to members of the public" also had the potential to influence service efficiency and should be considered grounds for dismissal (U.S. Merit Systems Protection Board, 2014). The courts seemed to align themselves with

Table 3.1 Chronology of Notable Legal Actions Affecting LGBTQ Employment

1953	Executive Order 10450, signed by President Eisenhower, listed "sexual perversion" as a potential means for dismissal due to potential conflicts with national security
1965	*Scott v Macy*, U.S. Court of Appeals for the District of Columbia ruled that the Civil Service Commission could not use "immoral" or "homosexual conduct" as a means to disqualify prospective federal employees
1969	*Norton v. Macy*, U.S. Court of Appeals for the District of Columbia ruled that Clifford Norton's employer (NASA) must establish a "rational basis" for his dismissal connects his conduct to service efficiency
1980	U.S. Office of Personnel Management declares the Civil Service Reform Act of 1978 applies to sexual orientation
1989	*Price Waterhouse v Hopkins*, U.S. Supreme Court ruled that discriminating against employees based on gender stereotypes violates Title VII of the Civil Rights Act of 1964
1995	Executive Order 12968, signed by President Clinton, prohibited government agencies from denying employees security clearances/classified information on the basis of their sexual orientation
1998	Executive Order 13087, signed by President Clinton, amended Executive Order 11478 and prohibited employment discrimination in the federal government based on sexual orientation
2012	*Macy v Department of Justice*, Equal Employment Opportunity Commission rules that discrimination against transgender employees violates Title VII of the Civil Rights Act of 1964
2020	*R.G. & G.R. Harris Funeral Homes Inc. v Equal Employment Opportunity Commission*, U.S. Supreme Court ruled that discriminating against transgender employees violates Title VII of the Civil Right Act of 1964
2020	*Bostock v Clayton County, Georgia*, U.S. Supreme Court ruled that discriminating against employees because of the sexual orientation or gender identity violates Title VII of the Civil Right Act of 1964

Macy's arguments, giving public agencies the ability to determine when efficiency of service was under threat. This discretion opened the possibility of federal employees being fired exclusively because of their sexual orientation, or suspicions surrounding their sexual orientation (U.S. Merit Systems Protection Board, 2014).

One of the most notable court cases helping to place LGBTQ employees outside of definitions of "good" public employees through the efficiency of service argument is *Norton v. Macy* (1969). In this case, Clifford Norton, a NASA employee was fired because of his sexuality. The Supreme Court actually ruled in favor of Norton, arguing that his firing was not justified (Lewis, 1997). However, the Court also argued that for Norton's dismissal to be justified, the government agency needs to provide evidence of a "rational nexus" between Norton's conduct and "efficiency of service" (Riccucci & Gossett, 1996). In sum, if an agency can draw a connection between an employee's sexuality and the reduced performance of the organization, they have grounds to dismiss that employee. At a time when homophobia was widespread and presidential candidates had campaign slogans that emphasized ridding public agencies of LGBTQ employees, providing a "rational nexus" between conduct and efficiency of service was not a difficult task. In addition, with Chairman Macy's comments that efficiency of service can be impacted by opinions of other employees and the general public toward LGBTQ employees, identifying grounds for dismissal was not a challenging barrier for agencies to overcome.

In 1970, the Eighth Circuit Court of Appeals ruled on *McConnell v. Anderson*. In this case, the court "upheld the denial of a university librarianship to an otherwise qualified [male] candidate solely because he applied for a license to marry another male, an event surrounded by a certain degree of local publicity" (Cain, 1993, p. 1578). McConnell's public role in advocating for gay rights was enough for the courts to decide that his dismissal was justified. Two years later, in 1972, the U.S. District Court for the District of Columbia decided *Richardson v. Hampton*. This case provides an example of a court finding that "homosexuality is persuasive evidence of a job applicant's unstable personality, which can negatively affect his or her job performance and hence service efficiency" (Riccucci & Gossett, 1996). McConnell was completing a one-year probationary appointment with the Post Office Department, and when interviewed by an investigator of the Civil Service Commission during his appointment, McConnell refused to answer questions about his private sexual life leading to his termination. While McConnell argued that his private sexual life was not the concern of his employer, the court denied McConnell's reinstatement of employment and argued:

> An employee's homosexual conduct may jeopardize the security of classified information because of the threat of blackmail, or it may in some circumstances be evidence of an unstable personality unsuited for particular kinds of work. In other instances a homosexual employee might engage in notorious and flagrant displays of unorthodox sexual behavior or make offensive overtures while on the job. Such conduct would certainly have a detrimental effect on other employees and the overall efficiency of the service.
>
> (McConnell, 345 F. Supp. 600 (D.D.C. 1972))

While the experiences of McConnell and Richardson provide examples of the courts siding with the Civil Service Commissions and upholding expectations of merit that allow for the exclusion of LGBTQ individuals from government employment, this changed in 1973 with the ruling on *Society for Individual Rights, Inc. v. Hampton*. In this case, the Court sought to reaffirm the ruling of *Norton v. Macy* and ensure that government employees were not being relieved of their positions solely because of their sexuality, but because of their job competence. More specifically, the Court deliberately rejected the Civil Service Commission's argument that employing gay, lesbian, and queer individuals would bring "public contempt" to the government and that this was grounds for their removal from government employment (U.S. Merit Systems Protection Board, 2014). This ruling was followed by a bulletin from the Civil Service Commission sent to all federal agencies, notifying them that homosexuality did not determine suitability of federal employment – the employee's sexual conduct must be connected to occupational competence and efficiency of service, which no longer included public contempt (Lewis, 1997).

A More Inclusive Meritocracy

From the 1960s to the 1990s, practitioner and academic understandings of merit began to expand and emphasize "social concerns related to fairness and equity" (Park & Liang, 2020, p. 85). However, in the 1960s, attempts to ground merit in the concepts of equity and fairness primarily focused on the experiences of women and people of color and attempting to increase their representation in government, not the LGBTQ community. It was not until 1975 that the federal government began to implement organizational policies that prohibited blatant discrimination against the LGBTQ community. Under pressure from the courts, the Civil Service Commission announced that government employees could not be dismissed from their roles because of sexual conduct that could bring contempt to the government – there must be evidence that the employee's conduct influences their occupational competence (U.S. Merit Systems Protection Board, 2014). Three years after this announcement from the Civil Service Commission, President Carter signed the Civil Service Reform Act (CSRA) of 1978. The CSRA dismantled the Civil Service Commission and largely shifted the functions of the Civil Service Commission to new administrative agencies, including the Office of Personnel Management. This shift signaled a move away from traditional understandings of merit and toward more political control of federal employment.

By examining the experience of the LGBTQ community in the public sector, it becomes apparent how our understanding of merit has evolved and changed as a means to both exclude and include certain groups. With respect to the LGBTQ community, there were 30 years of defining merit in narrower terms that would allow for their exclusion from the civil service because they were considered unsuitable for federal employment due to their sexual orientation. While the second core standard of the Pendleton Act, "prohibited firing federal employees for any reason other than cause" (Ingraham, 2006), key actors in the federal government changed the expectations of the meritocracy so cause against the LGBTQ community could be identified. It was not until the courts began to enforce two notable rulings (*Norton v. Macy* and *Society for Individual Rights, Inc. v. Hampton*), did understandings of merit in the federal government begin to change in a way that did not blatantly attempt to exclude LGBTQ employees by placing them outside of the requirements of suitable employees. In sum, the concept of merit has undergone many changes throughout its history, and many of those changes caused substantial harm to historically marginalized groups.

The 1960s and 1970s: The Compatibility of Merit and Equity

The Civil Rights Movement represents a turning point in American history. Taking place during the 1950s and 1960s, the Civil Rights Movement was led by notable activists and grassroots organizations with wide-ranging ideological perspectives on how to improve the standing of the Black community in the United States. The Civil Rights Movement reached its peak with the passing of the Civil Rights Act of 1964. The Civil Rights Act of 1964 is the result of "social, political, and legal forces" culminating to change the treatment of historically marginalized groups (Aiken, Salmon, & Hanges, 2013, p. 384). Title VII of The Civil Rights Act of 1964 is often the focus of public administration scholars since it formally prohibited workplace discrimination in the United States on the basis of race, color, religion, sex, or national origin. With the passing of this law, the expectation that the bureaucracy should reflect the communities it serves was codified, creating an explicit expectation of diversity and equity in government service. While the Civil Rights Act is one of the most recognized civil rights laws in American history, it remains one of many laws attempting to minimize the discrimination faced by marginalized groups. We discuss the role of law, and the myth of law, in creating more equitable employment in Chapter 5.

Toward the end of the Civil Rights Movement in 1968, Dwight Waldo organized a conference with the purpose of gathering younger scholars to explore the most pressing issues of the current time called Minnowbrook I (Wooldridge & Gooden, 2009; Gooden & Portillo, 2011). With the United States experiencing social and political unrest, conference attendees were tasked with exploring how the field of public administrator could contribute during such a tumultuous time (Gooden & Portillo, 2011). While scholars at Minnowbrook I put forth several ideas, arguably the most enduring was the concept of social equity put forth by H. George Frederickson. Social equity is linked to ideals of justice and fairness (Wooldridge & Gooden, 2009; Riccucci, 2009). As Frederickson (2010) notes, prior to the 1960s, the field of public administration was guided by the assumption that "good administration of government was equally good for everyone" (p. 75). However, during the 1960s, work from Civil Rights activists made it apparent that this was not the case. Certain policies and their implementation by government administrators were better for some than others in marginalized groups (Frederickson, 2010). As concerns of disparate treatment came to the forefront of scholarship and practice throughout the 1960s, desires for equity and bureaucratic representation increased, and were operationalized through the practices of equal employment opportunity and affirmative action (Riccucci, 1991).

The Merit-Equity Dichotomy

While the Civil Rights Act of 1964 is often the most recognized piece of legislation attempting to establish equity in the implementation of government policies and initiatives during the 1960s, presidents of this time also issued several Executive Orders in an attempt to improve the standing of women and people of color. In 1961, President Kennedy signed Executive Order 10925 that tasked federal contractors with taking "affirmative action" to ensure the fair treatment of applicants and employees regardless of their social identity (Reynolds, 1992). This was a notable action from the President since it was, "the first time that the government not only ordered its contractors to prevent discrimination, but to take steps to remedy the effects of past discrimination" (Ewoh & Elliott, 1997, p. 39).

Following President Kennedy's assassination, President Lyndon B. Johnson continued to work toward racial equity in the federal government. President Johnson issued Executive Orders 11246 and 11375 in 1965 and 1967, respectively (Ewoh & Elliott, 1997). A notable change took place in the implementation of affirmative action policies in 1971, when the U.S. Civil Service Commission began allowing "the use of goals and timetables for the hiring and promotion of women and members of certain minority groups for the first time" (Rosenbloom, 1984, p. 31). The incorporation of goals and timetables indicates that historically marginalized groups (i.e., women and people of color) will be given preference, leading opponents of affirmative action to suggest that policy implementation in this manner is not neutral and will discriminate against white men (Kellough, Coleman Selden, & Legge, 1997). Furthermore, opponents began to make claims that if affirmative action was used, many unqualified or less qualified women and people of color would enter into the civil service. For example, when reporting on affirmative action at universities, a piece from the New York Times stated, "The affirmative action program by which the Federal Government is compelling colleges and universities to hire more women and blacks is lowering standards and undermining faculty quality" (Maeroff, 1974). With the changes to affirmative action that took place in the early-1970s and the response that followed, the flawed logic of the equity-merit dichotomy began to take hold of the field.

There is a pattern of scholars, practitioners, and spectators of the public service, placing merit and equity in competition with one another – the argument goes if equity is improved, merit is being diminished and vice versa. This is known as the merit-equity dichotomy. This dichotomy goes beyond suggesting that these are concepts that struggle to coexist, but also highlights how scholars and practitioners often view these concepts as having an inverse relationship with one another – as one increases, the other decreases. While affirmative action policies sought to increase opportunities and representation of women and people of color in public organizations, overall, these policies garnered a significant negative response that has created several challenges for the groups they were intended to help. The negative response to affirmative action was made clear through court cases like *Regents of the University of California v. Bakke* that prohibited the use of racial quotas, and legislation like Proposition 209 in California that prohibited "affirmative action programs based on race, color, gender, ethnicity, or national origin in public hiring, contracting and college admissions" (Riccucci, 1997, p. 22). Arguments against affirmative action often center on their promotion of merit. However, the negative perception of affirmative action, with time, extended further and also impacted the way people saw diversity and equity more broadly. With certain affirmative action practices (i.e., quotas) being ruled as unconstitutional, there remains a stigma around the concepts of equity and diversity, so that people often view them as challenging merit.

It is, of course, important to point out that this dichotomy is a false one. Affirmative action policies, whether quotas or general calls for interviewing women or people of color for particular positions, have always stressed that candidates must be equally qualified. The goal is that qualified candidates who have traditionally been looked over or legally or illegally excluded from employment should have the consideration that they have historically been denied. However, the popular discussion of affirmative action continues to stress a dichotomy between equity and merit that implies candidates benefiting from a shift away from historical exclusion are somehow less than qualified.

Conclusion

In the imagination of most Americans, the idea of hiring, and promotion based on merit is connected to the belief that organizations should hire the best person for the job. On the face of things, we do not disagree with that position. However, deciding what counts as merit, and what does not, gets to be a bit trickier. Those who adopt the purist view of merit believe that we should make those decisions based on potential or prior performance, as determined by examinations-based methods, or other seemingly objective practices. However, we also know that the purist approach has never been the only approach and designing examination-based methods that are truly objective may be an unrealistic goal. We argue that employers and hiring managers have always been somewhat subjective in hiring and promotion practices. The definition of merit in American public administration hinges on the idea of who is seen as deserving in the eyes of those with decision-making power. This elevates the discussion of merit in public administration to the idea of myth. It has never truly been carried out in a pure way, but the way that merit is discussed within the field often obscures this fact. Hiring based on merit is a myth that we have told ourselves throughout our history, often hiding or ignoring explicit and implicit discrimination. In the following chapters, we continue to unpack the myths of our field, starting next with the myth of representation.

Works Cited

Cases

Scott v. Macy, 349 F.2d 182 (D.C. Cir. 1965). https://casetext.com/case/
scott-v-macy

Literature

Aiken, J. R., Salmon, E. D., & Hanges, P. J. (2013). The origins and legacy of the Civil Rights Act of 1964. *Journal of Business and Psychology, 28*(4), 383–399.

Anderson, J. F. (2013). The gospel according to merit: From virtue to rationality to production. *International Journal of Organization Theory & Behavior, 16*(4), 449–464.

Barnett, B. J. (2000). The US farm financial crisis of the 1980s. *Agricultural History, 74*(2), 366–380.

Cain, P. A. (1993). Litigating for lesbian and gay rights: A legal history. *Virginia Law Review, 79*(7), 1551–1641.

Demby, G. (2013). "The truth behind the lies of the original welfare queen" National Public Radio: www.npr.org/sections/codeswitch/2013/12/20/255819681/the-truth-behind-the-lies-of-the-original-welfare-queen

Elias, N. M. (2017). Constructing and implementing transgender policy for public administration. *Administration & Society, 49*(1), 20–47.

Ewoh, A. I. E., & Elliott, E. (1997). End of an era? Affirmative action and reaction in the 1990s. *Review of Public Personnel Administration, 17*(4), 38–51.

Executive Order 10450. (1953). "Security requirements for government employment".

Federman, P. S., & Rishel Elias, N. M. (2017). Beyond the lavender scare: LGBT and heterosexual employees in the federal workplace. *Public Integrity, 19*(1), 22–40.

Frederickson, G. (2010). *Social equity and public administration: Origins, developments, and applications.* Sharpe.

Gilliom, J. (2001). *Overseers of the poor: Surveillance, resistance, and the limits of privacy.* University of Chicago Press.

Gooden, S., & Portillo, S. (2011). Advancing social equity in the Minnowbrook tradition. *Journal of Public Administration Research and Theory, 21*(11), i61–i76.

Hancock, A. M. (2004). *The politics of disgust: The public identity of the welfare queen.* NYU Press.

Ingraham, P. W. (2006). Building bridges over troubled waters: Merit as a guide. *Public Administration Review, 66*(4), 486–495.

Kellough, J. E., Coleman Selden, S., & Legge, J. S. (1997). Affirmative action under fire: The current controversy and the potential for state policy retrenchment. *Review of Public Personnel Administration, 17*(4), 52–74.

King, D. S. (1995).*Separate and unequal: Black Americans and the US federal government.* Oxford University Press.

Krislov, S. (1964). *The Negro in federal employment: The quest for equal opportunity.* University of Minnesota Press.

Lewis, G. B. (1997). Lifting the ban on gays in the civil service: Federal policy toward gay and lesbian employees since the Cold War. *Public Administration Review, 57*(5), 387–395.

Maeroff, G. I. (1974, June 28). Minority hiring said to hurt colleges. *New York Times*. www.nytimes.com/1974/06/28/archives/minority-hiring-said-to-hurt-colleges.html

Marcus, C. R., & Otis, G. A. (2015). 'FDNY welcomes 305 rookie firefighters, including 3 women'. *Daily News*, 5.

Mosher, F. C. (1982). *Democracy and the public service*. Oxford University Press, USA.

Norton v. *Macy*, 417 F.2d 1161 (D.C. Cir. 1969). https://casetext.com/case/norton-v-macy

Park, S., & Liang, J. (2020). Merit, diversity, and performance: Does diversity management moderate the effect of merit principles on governmental performance? *Public Personnel Management*, *49*(1), 83–110.

Portillo, S., Bearfield, D., & Humphrey, N. (2020). The myth of bureaucratic neutrality: Institutionalized inequity in local government hiring. *Review of Public Personnel Administration*, *40*(3), 516–531.

Reynolds, W. B. (1992). Affirmative action and its negative repercussions. *The Annals of the American Academy of Political and Social Science*, *523*(1), 38–49.

Riccucci, N. M. (1991). Merit, equity, and test validity: A new look at an old problem. *Administration & Society*, *23*(1), 74–93.

———. (1997). The legal status of affirmative action: Past developments, future prospects. *Review of Public Personnel Administration*, *17*(4), 22–37.

———. (2009). The pursuit of social equity in the federal government: A road less traveled? *Public Administration Review*, *69*(3), 373–382.

Riccucci, N. M., & Gossett, C. W. (1996). Employment discrimination in state and local government: The lesbian and gay male experience. *American Review of Public Administration*, *26*(2), 175–200.

Rosenbloom, D. H. (1984). The declining salience of affirmative action in federal personnel management. *Review of Public Personnel Administration*, *4*(3), 31–40.

Santora, M., & Schwirtz, M. (2014). City settles lawsuit accusing fire dept. of racial bias. *New York Times*, 19.

Schneider, A., & Ingram, H. (1993). Social construction of target populations: Implications for politics and policy. *American Political Science Review*, *87*(2), 334–347.

U.S. Merit Systems Protection Board. (2014). *Sexual orientation and the federal workplace: Policy and perception*. A Report to the President and Congress by the U.S. Merit Systems Protection Board: https://www.mspb.gov/studies/studies/Sexual_Orientation_and_the_Federal_Workplace_Policy_Perception_1026379.pdf

Van Riper, P. P. (1958). *History of the United States civil service*. Row and Peterson Publishing.

Woodard, C. A. (2005). Merit by any other name: Reframing the civil service first principle. *Public Administration Review*, *65*(1), 109–116.

Wooldridge, B., & Gooden, S. (2009). The epic of social equity: Evolution, essence, and emergence. *Administrative Theory & Praxis*, *31*(2), 222–234.

4   The Myth of Representation

On May 25, 2020, George Floyd was detained by four police officers after he was accused of trying to use a counterfeit 20-dollar bill at a local convenience store in Minneapolis, Minnesota. After he was handcuffed, with his hands behind his back, the officers held Floyd on the ground for approximately 8 minutes and 46 seconds (Bogel-Burroughs, 2020). One officer, Derek Chauvin, placed his knee on Mr. Floyd's neck as Floyd repeatedly tried to tell the officers that he could not breathe. According to police body camera footage, following their arrival, medical personnel did not begin treatment on Mr. Floyd for three minutes. He was pronounced dead about an hour later (Bailey, 2020).

Based on his actions when interacting with Mr. Floyd, Officer Chauvin was arrested on May 29, 2020 and charged with second-degree murder and manslaughter. According to news reports, Black sergeant proceeded to pat down officer Chauvin for weapons, a standard operating procedure for incoming inmates. In the middle of the pat down, he was told by a superior that he was not to do the pat down or escort Chauvin to his cell. It was later revealed the superintendent of the jail made the decision that correctional officers of color would not be allowed to interact with Officer Chauvin. Officers of color were removed from their normal duties and replaced with white officers (Gottfried, 2020; Sawyer, 2020).

During an internal investigation, Officer Lydon, the officer in charge of the order, suggested that officers of color may have suffered "acute racialized trauma" from Floyd's death and that he removed the officers in an attempt to protect them. He also noted that the officers were not removed over safety concerns for Chauvin or questions over the professionalism of the officers. No one could recall a time when white officers were removed in similar situations (Sawyer, 2020). As we discussed in Chapter 1, the myth of neutrality has been institutionalized in our field based on white, masculine, and heterosexual norms. In this chapter,

DOI: 10.4324/9781003322795-4

we consider how the myth of representation in public administration reinforces that idea.

So, what is it about the arrest of Officer Derek Chauvin that would cause the removal of qualified officers of color from a detail of national significance? According to a Black acting sergeant working on the Chauvin detail, "I understood that the decision to segregate us had been made because we could not be trusted to carry out our work responsibilities professionally around the high-profile inmate – solely because of the color of our skin" (Sawyer, 2020). It is our contention, that more often than not, if public administration scholars were to explore this case, they would avoid addressing this issue head-on, because it deals with blatant racism.

Racism is something the field tends to avoid (Gooden, 2015; Starke et al., 2018). Instead, public administration scholars often focus on representative bureaucracy as a means to study race issues. While representative bureaucracy is an important area of study, it does not effectively address racism. Within the context of this example, scholars would look to see if there are enough officers of color at the jail to advocate for better treatment for themselves and inmates of color. Alternatively, they might question if the lack of Black officers impacts the legitimacy of the organization among Black constituents. While these are important questions to consider, they also avoid exploring the most pressing questions: are these workers being discriminated against because of their race, and why were they not trusted to be neutral, objective professionals?

Scholars such as Stivers (2007), Alexander (1997), and Witt (2006) have all described the field's reluctance to engage the idea that racism is used by some public administrators to shape administrative decisions and policy implementation. We charge that because it is an uncomfortable conversation, the field has moved away from exploring issues of discrimination directly. Instead, scholars of public administration favor discussions of representative bureaucracy, with a focus on identity matching, rather than discrimination and racism. Stated another way, when we witness discrimination against marginalized communities, we tend to avoid grappling with tough issues, such as racism, sexism, or homophobia, and other forms of discrimination. Instead, we emphasize the need for more representation of historically marginalized groups. But representation and racism can coexist. Representation, while important, only addresses part of the issue and allows us to avoid topics that make us "nervous" or may spark real discussions of change. When an instance of discrimination occurs, and we primarily focus on conversations of representation to address the issue, we avoid direct discussions of how racism, sexism, and homophobia may have influenced the organization and its administrators' actions. It is uncomfortable to explicitly talk about discrimination, and the field has become, as Gooden (2014) would say, "nervous."

This nervousness has led to discussions of representation and representative bureaucracy serving as a stand in for discussions of racism. Discussions of representative bureaucracy are often seen as positive because they focus on diversifying public service and ensuring public servants reflect the communities they serve. The point here is not to disparage one of the most important developments in our field. Instead, we suggest the narrow focus of representative bureaucracy on people of color and women, and the overreliance on representative bureaucracy as a singular framework to understand race and gender in our field, has created a blind spot that thwarts our ability to understand longstanding and ongoing systemic racial and gender discrimination. In fact, in recent years, representative bureaucracy has emerged as a dominant approach for empirical examinations of race, gender, ethnicity, and sexual orientation in the field (Bearfield, 2014). However, a focus on increasing the representation of marginalized communities without critiquing the actions of organizations can hide or normalize assumptions about whiteness, masculinity, and heteronormativity in public organizations. The focus on representation, which often emphasizes discussions of hiring and individual decision-making by administrators, allows us to avoid institutional level discussions focused on how racism, sexism, or homophobia may be a broader part of organizational policies, practices, and institutionalized behavior. By overlooking institutionalized discriminatory behavior, we fail to see the way whiteness and masculinity permeate organizations and permit discriminatory practices. Our goal is to push the field to consider the ways we fail to hold bureaucrats accountable for not serving historically marginalized citizens, clients, and employees.

In this chapter, we use representative bureaucracy as a lens to explore how public administration often avoids discussions of whiteness and masculinity, and the implications this has for our understanding of diversity and equity in the public sector. We go on to suggest a focus on accountability and potentially compensating public servants to directly address inequalities and racial diversity within public organizations. Ultimately, to progress our understanding and commitment to equity as a field, we must acknowledge how race and gender have influenced the practice and scholarship of public administration in the United States, which can only happen by gaining insight on the implicit influence of whiteness and masculinity in our field.

Representative Bureaucracy Scholarship

Representative bureaucracy has emerged as a major area of study in public administration. Originally conceived by Kingsley to grapple with the lack of class and gender representation in the British civil service system (1944), it has since been adopted by a host of scholars looking to apply it in an American context (Van Riper, 1958; Mosher, 1982). In the 1950s and 1960s, Van Riper (1958) and Krislov (1967) understood that representative bureaucracy could also be used to explore the under-representation of racial minorities, specifically Black constituents, in American public sector positions. In the years that followed, representative bureaucracy has been used to explore issues related to gender and/or racial representation at the federal (Meier, Pennington, & Eller 2005), state (Riccucci & Saidel, 1997), and local levels (Goode & Baldwin, 2005; Meier & Wilkins, 2002).

Representative bureaucracy theory assumes bureaucratic organizations that reflect their constituents will reflect the interests of those constituents (Kingsley, 1944; Krislov, 1974). Research has explored this assumption through two forms of representation, passive and active. Passive representation describes reflecting constituents' demographic traits (Selden, 1997; Sowa & Selden, 2003). Active representation moves beyond reflecting constituents demographically and emphasizes attempting to reflect constituents' interests (Keiser, Wilkins, Meier, & Holland, 2002). Mosher (1968) helped provide the distinction between passive and active representation (Rosenbloom & Featherstonhaugh, 1977). Building on Mosher's discussion, several studies have been able to draw a link between passive and active representation, finding that people of color (Meier & Stewart, 1992; Meier et al., 1999) and women (Keiser et al., 2002; Wilkins & Keiser, 2006) can improve outcomes for groups sharing their identities.

Along with passive and active representation, scholars have also begun giving attention to symbolic representation. This form of representation suggests that the mere presence of historically underrepresented groups can improve constituent perceptions of the bureaucracy. For example, research on veterans (Gade & Wilkins, 2012), and the police (Riccucci et al., 2018), indicate that constituents view bureaucracies more favorably when they socially identify with members of the organization, even if the public servants are not taking direct actions to represent their interests. Stated another way, we still see improved bureaucratic outcomes with symbolic representation, even when public servants do not take direct action. Their passive representation in the organization leads to more favorable perceptions of the organization among constituents. Recent literature has added significant developments to the field's understanding of symbolic representation, highlighting the importance of identity and individual lived experience (Headley et al., 2021).

While several studies have demonstrated a correlation between passive and active representation, scholars should not take this relationship for granted (Mosher, 1968). There are multiple factors that can enhance or diminish the link between passive and active representation. Several studies have found that public servants are more likely to participate in active representation when a critical number of marginalized individuals are in the organization (Hindera, 1993; Selden, 1997; Nicholson-Crotty, Nicholson-Crotty, & Fernandez, 2017). This suggests, "the representativeness of the bureaucracy can affect bureaucratic responsiveness to identifiable segments of the population" (Selden, 1997). Additionally, administrative discretion plays an important role in active representation. Specifically, administrators that perceive themselves as having more discretion are more likely to pursue outcomes improving outcomes for marginalized groups (Sowa & Seldon, 2003). In short, prior research highlights that active representation is at least partially dependent on the overall presence of public servants in the organization identifying with the group being served and administrative discretion.

Implicit Problems with the Logic of Representation

Representative bureaucracy represents a pillar of research in the field of public administration that has made several contributions to our understanding of equity and diversity in the public sector. At the same time, representative bureaucracy establishes a logic of understanding that implicitly establishes white men as neutral and objective actors, while placing the burden of resolving equity issues on historically marginalized groups. Our focus in this chapter is to explore whiteness and masculinity in connection to representative bureaucracy literature, and more broadly public administration scholarship. We aim to bring attention to assumptions that have been developed by avoiding critical and empirical investigations regarding the latent presence of whiteness and masculinity. By recognizing how these qualities have shaped our scholarship and practice, we can gain a more comprehensive understanding of race, gender, and sexual orientation in the context of public sector organizations. Below we walk through these two major concerns – whiteness and masculinity as neutral and the increased burden on the already marginalized – before turning to potential solutions for scholarship and practice.

White Men as Objective and Neutral

As we discussed in Chapter 2, in public administration scholarship masculinity has historically been held up as the norm (Bishu, Guy, & Heckler, 2019). From discussions on how to end the administrative man (Denhardt & Perkins, 1976), to more current research focused on how to decenter masculinity from human research policies in public organizations (Mastracci & Arreola, 2016), it is apparent that masculinity is deeply connected to the field's understanding of public servants. This is echoed by Stivers (2002) who argued that public administration as a field of study and practice is gendered toward masculinity.

Coupled with the underlying presence of masculinity is whiteness. Whiteness represents the social and legal benefits granted to individuals and groups that are allowed to identify as white (Brown et al., 2003). The term "allowed" is central to this definition of whiteness because for several immigrants in the United States, identifying as white took time (Roediger, 2005). Whiteness is considered valuable (Brown et al., 2003), in the United States and several other countries and cultures. Because of this, whiteness involves gatekeeping with groups of people utilizing color, ethnicity, and geography to ensure the benefits of whiteness are maintained only by those "allowed" to identify as white. Historically, research has centered on the assumption of whiteness as the norm in organizational settings (Nkomo, 1992; Ferguson, 1984). As Heckler (2017) describes, whiteness is, "part of the institutional setting of public organizations" (p. 176). As part of the institutional setting, it creates prescriptions on how public employees should conduct themselves (Heckler, 2017). This has helped to establish whiteness as a taken-for-granted latent quality in organizations (Macalpine & Marsh, 2005). Together, these two traits – masculinity and whiteness – create a proto-type for public servants.

Holding whiteness and masculinity as the standard has consequences for employees that do not align with these qualities. Research on role congruity has provided one of the most robust avenues of research on this topic. Role congruency theory suggests that incongruence between stereotypes of a social group and assumed prototypic behavior of specific organizational roles leads to prejudice (Eagly & Karau, 2002). Looking at the experience of women in organizations settings, role congruity scholarship indicates that managerial positions are often associated with masculinity, and because women are expected to present feminine traits that are often perceived as incongruent with managerial roles, they tend to be evaluated more harshly than men occupying similar positions (Funk, 2019; Eagly & Karau, 2002). In addition, research focused on racial role congruence has found that compared to white employees, employees of color are viewed as incongruent with managerial positions (Chung-Herrera & Lankau, 2005; Rosette, Leonardelli, & Phillips, 2008; Sy et al., 2010), and jobs requiring certain types of emotional displays, such as warmth (Grandey, Houston, & Avery, 2019). The perceived incongruence of women and people of color with certain organizational positions can lead to harsher evaluations and reduced opportunities. In sum, holding whiteness and masculinity as the standard is not simply a normative question of right and wrong, but is a practical question with real consequences for those in minoritized positions.

This practice of holding whiteness and masculinity as the base for comparison is often implicitly reflected in representative bureaucracy literature. Because whiteness and masculinity have traditionally and presumptively been seen as neutral, white and male bureaucrats have largely not been linked to outcomes for community members aligning with their identities. As a result, white men emerge as the standard against which everyone else is compared. Representative bureaucracy often falls into the myth of neutrality (Portillo, Bearfield, & Humphrey, 2020), which presents white men as neutral and objective, while *others* are presumed to be biased and subjective.

In short, what we often see in the literature is white normativity, or the idea that certain "cultural norms and practices" exist that allow whiteness to appear as the standard or right (Ward, 2008). To address white normativity, scholarship suggests "interrogating whiteness" (Grimes, 2002); through interrogation, identifying and questioning assumptions about whiteness that are often latent in practice and research (Grimes, 2002). In addition, this process allows us to explore how whiteness has become institutionalized in our organizations, even when they are racially diverse. By focusing on, "white norms and white culture, it becomes possible to consider whether organizational cultures may reflect the interpretive frames of whites, even when organizational participants and leaders are racially diverse and share antiracist values" (Ward, 2008, p. 564). Moving forward, it is important that we as a field begin to question how whiteness underlies our research and practice.

Similarly, scholars invite us to consider how organizations are gendered (Acker, 2006). Stivers has argued that as a field, we have focused on the masculine nature of public service since our very founding (2002). More recently scholars have asserted that we have become oblivious to the ways that gender is infused within public organizations (Doan & Portillo, 2019). Ultimately, masculinity and whiteness blend into the organization, reinforcing the idea of women and people of color as "other" and outsiders in the field.

The Burden of the Historically Marginalized

The second implicit problem emphasizes how discussions on representative bureaucracy can place the burden of resolving equity issues on historically marginalized groups. Bureaucrats of color, in much of the representative bureaucracy scholarship, are presented as serving all constituents, but especially improving outcomes for clients of color (Meier, Wrinkle, & Polinard, 1999). In linking bureaucrats of color to outcomes for clients and citizens of color, while decoupling white male bureaucrats from outcomes of marginalized community members, we have inadvertently reinforced the idea that white bureaucrats will not serve all clients effectively, and it is the sole responsibility of marginalized groups to correct inequalities.

While the representation of historically marginalized groups is important and has been shown to improve outcomes for underrepresented groups (Meier & Stewart, 1992; Meier, 1993; Meier et al., 1999; Keiser et al., 2002; Wilkins & Keiser, 2006), they cannot be looked at as the only groups responsible for solving decades of oppression and discrimination. It implies white men are incapable, or at least reluctant to provide fair service to all constituents. As a result, we must hire *others* to deal with the problem. We are not arguing that bringing marginalized people into the organization is a bad thing. However, it is concerning that marginalized people are viewed as the only people capable of resolving inequalities, which have indeed been created by organizations overwhelmingly led by bureaucrats who are white. This places a specific burden on bureaucrats of color – to be the individuals responsible for addressing inequity and systems of oppression in their organizations.

Research has found that in some situations, public servants treat clients they share demographic qualities with more harshly, out of fear they will be perceived as unprofessional for favoring clients they demographically identify with (Watkins-Hayes, 2011). In these instances, attempting to provide compassion or sympathy contradicts foundational ideals of public administration that emphasize objectivity and neutrality (Thompson, 1975). In other cases, individuals with limited discretion may not have the flexibility to address the challenges faced by clients in their kinship or affinity group. This indicates that historically marginalized public servants may not feel as though they can work in the interest of constituents they identify with. Individuals identifying with traditionally marginalized groups, "carry the burden of having to choose between tacitly participating in their marginalization or actively resisting racist ideologies with the possible consequence of institutional alienation, exclusion, or official reprimand" (Evans & Moore, 2015).

In short, while marginalized groups provide valuable contributions on behalf of marginalized communities, efforts to address inequity must be widespread throughout the organization.

It is possible to read our interpretation of the literature as a revival of the debate between universal versus particularistic managerial paradigm. Traditionally universalism is an attempt to apply the same standard to everyone, while particularism embraces the approach that there can be different standards for different groups depending on the circumstances (Thompson & Hoggett, 1996). It is easy to walk away with the impression that white bureaucrats tend to favor applying the same standards to all clients, while bureaucrats of color favor applying particularistic standards to some clients, notably clients of color. Instead, we put forth a different interpretation. As it stands, we argue that because the motivations of white male bureaucrats have largely gone unexamined, the representative bureaucracy literature is vulnerable to the charge of protecting a veiled form of particularism. In this respect, white male bureaucrats are able to provide particularistic benefits to other white males, while giving off the appearance of applying universal standards to everyone. This risk remains as long as we ignore how white males engage in representative bureaucracy in favor of primarily examining the behavior of people of color.

Within the field, representative bureaucracy scholarship began by examining the behavior and outcomes of bureaucrats of color and women, the "others" in organizations, without any real analysis of the norm – white male bureaucrats. This has centered the discussion of representation on minoritized communities, without fully understanding how privileged communities have been represented throughout the history of our field.

Viewing Representative Bureaucracy in Reverse

Representative bureaucracy literature has consistently found that women and bureaucrats of color act in ways that benefit other women and people of color. While this may reflect selection bias in the publication process, where journals are more likely to publish positive results, it is important that we consider this finding in reverse, acknowledging that white males are also likely to provide benefits for those they socially align with. A question that is worth additional consideration is whether or not white men are capable of improving outcomes for others, while providing benefits to those they identify with. Although women and bureaucrats of color have been found to improve outcomes for clients of similar identities, research has also noted their ability to improve outcomes for all constituents (Meier et al., 1999). This is not a question that has been regularly asked of white men but is essential to gaining a deeper understanding of inequity.

Following a substantial amount of research in the 1990s indicating that bureaucrats of color improved the experiences of constituents of color, people began to question if these benefits were achieved at the expense of the majority group, white constituents. While the literature has shown this is not the case (Meier et al., 1999; Hong, 2017), it is concerning that this is a question that has been asked of traditionally marginalized groups, and not those holding privileged positions. Women and people of color have the expectation to improve outcomes for those they identify with, while still effectively serving everyone. This is not something we have traditionally asked of their white male counterparts. When pressed, it is quite possible that the field is not interested in how white males engage in active participation. It seems so obvious that white men, like any other interest group, would act on behalf of white men. Yet, if our goal is to deepen our understanding of active representation, we cannot allow a combination of myth, folklore, and unfounded assumptions to stand in place for empirical investigation.

What Is the Alternative?

Discussions of accountability are inherent in discussions of representative bureaucracy scholarship. People of color and women are often the focus of this scholarship and are often seen demonstrating improved outcomes for constituents they represent, while not sacrificing services for individuals who hold more traditionally privileged identities – white men. While the empirical literature does not suggest that women and minorities must improve these outcomes, we contend that in practice, bureaucrats from marginalized populations are under pressure to "represent."

We present two alternatives for how the field might address the myth of representation. First, we make the discussion of accountability explicit and apply it to all members of the organization. This would mean holding administrators who are othered and administrators who are privileged accountable for outcomes for all constituents. Given the broad discretion that many administrators have in performing their jobs, we must make space to examine when administrators fail to deliver positive outcomes for specific populations. It is possible that administrators may be successful in serving the larger white population, while coming up short when it comes to people of color. Moving forward, we need to identify both when that occurs and why. Once it is identified, managers can then apply the appropriate remedy, from training, to sanction, to removal, in an effort to improve outcomes for all constituents.

Alternatively, organizations and administrators can recognize the unique skills and abilities that administrators who have been historically "othered" bring to their role and compensate them for the improved outcomes for constituents they represent. This means acknowledging the increased labor that bureaucrats of color and women are performing when they are being asked to represent and paying them for that labor. We address both alternatives below, noting that these are not set up as dichotomous, and may both be implemented as part of a comprehensive response to the myth of representation in our field.

Going back to its founding, representative bureaucracy scholarship argued that public servants should reflect the communities they serve. This was initially an argument that rested on theories of democracy, a representative administrative state should mirror the demos or people they are serving. But eventually, the argument morphed into discussions of effectiveness. Scholars argued that in order to be effective, organizations needed a diverse workforce. A diversity of lived experiences and viewpoints would help organizations better serve the public. Both of these notions rest on the normative idea that diverse representation adds value to an organization and yields positive outcomes. Diversity management scholars have empirically studied the positive benefits of a diverse workforce (Wise & Tschirhart, 2000; Ewoh, 2013). However, this scholarship, much like the representative bureaucracy scholarship focuses on the addition of people of color and women in organizations. Again, this reinforces the point that serving the interests of minoritized citizens, or clients, is a responsibility best shouldered by minoritized bureaucrats.

In his critique of the implementation of affirmative action, Skrentny (2015) argues that organizations practice a kind of racial realism. While the law provides only very limited considerations for how race may be used as a factor in hiring, organizations actually rely on race in very specific ways. Skrentny (2015) used data from public and private organizations to argue that employers use race in four distinct ways. Racial matching – that clients of color may be more likely to relate to employees of color, so organizations benefit when their workforce mirrors their clients. Diversity – having a more diverse workforce protects against groupthink and is linked to better outcomes. Signaling – having a diverse workforce communicates something to constituents and clients, the organization demonstrates its values via its workforce and hiring practices. Racial characteristics – employers may hold stereotypes about workers' abilities based on their race. Beyond just matching, employers may hold stereotyped views about workers that lead them to hire based on particular groups. These stereotypes may be perceived as positive – a particular racial group being perceived as hardworking – but nonetheless, they are stereotypes of groups placed on individuals.

According to Skrentny (2015), racial realism is a recognition of how race actually functions in modern organizations – race in action rather than race in the abstract. This approach is fundamentally different from how we read about race, particularly in the law. Law functions to tell us how we should not consider race when it comes to hiring decisions, but Skrentny's work is largely focused on how modern employers actually do consider and use race within organizations. This is a critique of how modern interpretations of employment law have not kept up with how race functions in organizations, but the concepts are relevant to representative bureaucracy theory and our discussion of the myth of representation.

In particular, the idea of racial matching parallels the idea of representative bureaucracy theory. Similar to representative bureaucracy scholars, Skrentny (2015) presents significant empirical evidence across a number of industries backing up the real benefits of racial matching for the outcomes of organizations. When organizations have workforces that match their client base, they have better desired outcomes. However, he critiques this practice on a number of grounds. First, it is not how civil rights law was intended. Taking race into account when selecting from qualified candidates and giving preference to qualified candidates from traditionally marginalized backgrounds, was meant to correct historical wrongs, and be temporary. Affirmative action focused on creating spaces for Black workers and women who had been historically kept out of professionalized workplaces but had the same qualifications and skills as their white male counterparts. These policies were meant to correct the wrongs of institutionalized racism and sexism without a focus on the outcomes of organizations. The law was focused on individual opportunities that were limited because of historic racism. Rather than focusing on individual opportunity, organizations are instead using race as a factor in discussing outcomes of the organization. Not focusing on past injustice, but instead on future productivity.

Even if we set aside the legal and ethical aspects of this choice, it often leads to worse assignments for employees of color. Improved outcomes for the organization may not result in improved outcomes for the individual. For example, police officers of color may be assigned to patrol areas that have been historically redlined and under-resourced. These areas, which may have more residents of color, are also less affluent and patrol officers working in these areas are more likely to burn out and less likely to move up from patrol to administrative positions. By assigning historically marginalized employees to serve the most historically underserved, organizations are perpetuating systemic discrimination, not ending it.

Skrentny (2015) does a magnificent job of walking through the legal history and current realities of the modern-day workplace. He demonstrates that the way racial realism functions in the workplace is well outside of the expectations and intentions of employment law. While the law is focused on correcting past wrongs, current racial practices in organizations focus on future outcomes. However, he also argues that governments and public organizations have implicitly endorsed ideas of racial realism through their rhetoric around diversity and hiring initiatives. Calls for diversity in hiring, and campaigns to make public employment more reflective of American communities, demonstrate that racial realism is valued, at least rhetorically, by public officials and community leaders. Governments and public organizations regularly engage in what Skrenty (2015) refers to as racial signaling. Holding up hires, potentially in a tokenized fashion, to demonstrate a commitment to diversity, even if that commitment does not extend to correcting historic discrimination and institutionalized racism.

Skrenty (2015) ultimately provides language to describe the nuanced ways that modern organizations rely on racialized labor. It is this naming of racialized labor that is the core of his concept of racial realism and is relevant for discussions of the myth of representation in public administration. While we traditionally hold up representation as a positive thing within our field, we rarely interrogate how it works and if it truly addresses our goals regarding equity in service delivery and workplace experiences.

As a field, we regularly discuss effectiveness and efficiency. According to Stivers (2000), Progressive reformers focused on an instrumental definition of efficiency, with a primary focus on reducing waste, and stretching resources so that they could serve the needs of the community. In fact, Waldo (1974) points out that efficiency has taken on a moral significance, one that equates good service with efficient service. However, foundational terms that leave out explicit discussions of identity and often focus on doing the job devoid of representation. Here the idea is that efficiency means public administrators can serve everyone in the community, and they are accountable for effective services throughout the communities they work in. True accountability may mean that representation does not matter, but outcomes for all constituents do. However, recognizing that representation may have a measurable effect on outcomes means that what Skrentny (2015) refers to as racial realism may be monetizable skills. If equity is also a goal of good bureaucracies, then compensating for representation as a unique skill within the organization would make logical sense.

While these may sound like dichotomous options – accountability to all constituents regardless of organizational representation or acknowledgement of racial realism and compensation for it, this does not have to be an either/or choice. Organizations may do both, recognize racial abilities and compensate them accordingly *and* work toward holding all workers accountable for equitable service. Both approaches recognize and address the myth of representation. Both approaches also demand that public organizations take on the task of discussing racialized outcomes and processes directly – confronting the nervous area of government (Gooden, 2014).

Conclusion

Representative bureaucracy scholarship has traditionally focused on the representation of people traditionally seen as *other* in the modern professional workforce – people of color and women. In this chapter, we have argued that while whiteness, masculinity, and heterosexuality are explicitly absent from discussions of representative bureaucracy, they often have a veiled presence in our research with implications for the field of public administration. They are the norm that representation is judged against. Our purpose in this chapter was to present the myth of representation – the assumption that only bureaucrats of the same background can provide efficient, effective, and equitable services in diverse democratic communities. The myth of representation masks the structural inequalities built into our bureaucratic organizations, placing the burden of fixing these inequalities on bureaucrats who have been historically marginalized. This allows us, as a field, to avoid "nervous" areas of discussion. In short, we can avoid explicit discussions of racism, sexism, homophobia, and other forms of discrimination that may be present in public organizations.

Equally important, research in public administration has lost its way over time. In order to truly understand why women, people of color, and other marginalized groups are underrepresented in the workforce, we must do more to lay out the historical and legal case that produced the inequality. Van Riper (1958), Krislov (1967), Meier, Stewart, and England (1989), and Riccucci and Saidel (1997) all took the care to explain that inequalities did not just happen by accident. It must be said that much of the lack of representation in public sector organizations are the result of legal, cultural, and local administrative decisions that prioritized white males over others, despite their inability to serve the entire public or the entirety of their organization. Without this context, readers are left with an incomplete understanding of the systemic problem of underrepresentation – as if women, and people of color, were left out by accident, or even worse, as a result of their own decision-making. As a field of practice, it is tremendously important to be clear not only in what we say, but also in what we mean. Scholars of representative bureaucracy have done a tremendous job in highlighting the inequalities in public organizations. As practitioners look to this body of research for ideas on how to make their organizations more representative, the need to be explicit about what we mean, and what we do not, becomes abundantly clear.

Finally, while the work of historically marginalized groups is important, addressing structural inequalities in bureaucratic organizations must be the work of all public servants. Rather than relying exclusively on increasingly diverse hiring to remedy disparities in outcomes for people of color and women, organizations should recognize that white men have traditionally been represented, likely giving them generations of privileged outcomes in public organizations. Organizations must recognize this historical representation of white men in order to truly address how we might move toward more equitable outcomes for all constituents. Two practical responses include holding all public administrators accountable for serving all constituents and recognizing and compensating the racial and gender abilities of administrators who have been traditionally othered in our field.

In the following chapter discuss our final myth – the myth of legal remedies. We argue that law has long been held up as a solution to discrimination in employment; however, it has not been the panacea many hoped for. Following the discussion of our final myth, we present an alternative to representation as a remedy to current inequalities. We suggest that a historically grounded positionality would allow us to fully address where inequalities come from in our field as well as how bureaucrats can recognize their own role in correcting them. Without understanding the history of inequities, public servants are not fully prepared to correct them.

Works Cited

Acker, J. (2006). Inequality regimes: Gender, class, and race in organizations. *Gender &Society*, *20*(4), 441–464.

Alexander, J. (1997). Avoiding the issue: Racism and administrative responsibility in public administration. *The American Review of Public Administration*, *27*(4), 343–361.

Bailey, H. (2020). George Floyd warned police he thought he would die because he couldn't breathe, according to body camera transcripts. *Washington Post*.

Bearfield, D. A. (2014). 'It's been a long time coming': An examination of public personnel research in PAR and ROPPA in celebration of the fiftieth anniversary of the civil rights act of 1964. *Review of Public Personnel Administration*, *34*(1), 59–74.

Bishu, S. G., Guy, M. E., & Heckler, N. (2019). Seeing gender and its consequences. *Journal of Public Affairs Education*, *25*(2), 145–162.

Bogel-Burroughs, N. (2020). 8 minutes, 46 seconds became a symbol in George Floyd's death. The exact time is less clear. *New York Times, 18* www.nytimes.com/2020/06/18/us/george-floyd-timing.html

Brown, Michael K., Martin Carnoy, Elliott Currie, Troy Duster, David B. Oppenheimer, Majorie M. Shultz, and David Wellman. 2003. *Whitewashing race: The myth of a color-blind society*. University of California Press

Chung-Herrera, B. G., & Lankau, M. J. (2005). Are we there yet? An assessment of fit between stereotypes of minority managers and the successful-manager prototype. *Journal of Applied Social Psychology*, *35*(10), 2029–2056.

Denhardt, R. B., & Perkins, J. (1976). The coming of death of administrative man. *Public Administration Review*, *36*(4), 379–384.

Doan, A., & Portillo, S. (2019). *Organizational obliviousness: Entrenched resistance to gender integration in the military*. Cambridge: Cambridge University Press.

Eagly, A. H., & Karau, S. J. (2002). Role congruity theory of prejudice toward female leaders. *Psychological Review*, *109*(3), 573.

Evans, L., & Moore, W. L. (2015). Impossible burdens: White institutions, emotional labor, and micro-resistance. *Social Problems*, *62*(3), 439–454.

Ewoh, A. I. (2013). Managing and valuing diversity: Challenges to public managers in the 21st century. *Public Personnel Management*, *42*(2), 107–122.

Ferguson, K. (1984). *The feminist case against bureaucracy*. Philadelphia, PA: Temple University Press.

Funk, K. (2019). If the shoe fits: Gender role congruity and evaluations of public managers. *Journal of Behavioral Public Administration*, *2*(1). https://doi.org/10.30636/jbpa.21.48

Gade, D. M., & Wilkins, V. M. (2012). Where did you serve? Veteran identity, representative bureaucracy, and vocational rehabilitation. *Journal of Public Administration Research and Theory*, *23*(2), 267–288.

Goode, S. J., & Baldwin, J. N. (2005). Predictors of African American representation in municipal government. *Review of Public Personnel Administration*, *25*(1), 29–55.

Gooden, S. T. (2015). *Race and social equity: A nervous area of government*. Routledge.

Gottfried, M. (2020). *Correctional officers of color who say they were segregated from Derek Chauvin: Why isn't Ramsey County jail superintendent on leave?* www.twincities.com/2020/07/07/correctional-officers-of-color-who-say-they-were-segregated-from-derek-chauvin-why-isnt-ramsey-co-jail-superintendent-on-leave/

Grandey, A. A., Houston, L., & Avery, D. R. (2019). Fake it to make it? Emotional labor reduces the racial disparity in service performance judgments. *Journal of Management*, *45*(5), 2163–2192.

Grimes, D. S. (2002). Challenging the status quo? Whiteness in the diversity management literature. *Management Communication Quarterly*, *15*(3), 381–409.

Headley, A. M., Wright, J. E., & Meier, K. J. (2021). Bureaucracy, democracy, and race: the limits of symbolic representation. *Public Administration Review*, *81*(6), 1033–1043.

Heckler, N. (2017). Publicly desired color-blindness: Whiteness as a realized public value. *Administrative Theory & Praxis*, *39*(3), 175–192.

Hindera, J. J. (1993). Representative bureaucracy: Further evidence of active representation in the EEOC district offices. *Journal of Public Administration Research and Theory*, *3*(4), 415–429.

Hong, S. (2017). Does increasing ethnic representativeness reduce police misconduct? *Public Administration Review*, *77*(2), 195–205.

Keiser, L., Wilkins, V., Meier, K., & Holland, C. (2002). Lipstick and logarithms: Gender, institutional context, and representative bureaucracy. *American Political Science Review*, *96*(3), 553–565.

Kingsley, J. D. (1944). *Representative bureaucracy: An interpretation of the British civil service*. Antioch Press.

Krislov, S. (1967). *The Negro in federal employment: The quest for equal opportunity*. University of Minnesota Press.

———. (1974). *Representative bureaucracy*. Prentice Hall.

Macalpine, M., & Marsh, S. (2005). "On being white: There's nothing I can say": Exploring whiteness and power in organizations. *Management Learning*, *36*(4), 429–450.

Mastracci, S., & Arreola, V. I. (2016). Gendered organizations: How human resource management practices produce and reproduce administrative man. *Administrative Theory & Praxis*, *38*(2), 137–149.

Meier, K. J. (1993). Latinos and representative bureaucracy: Testing the Thompson and Henderson hypotheses. *Journal of Public Administration Research and Theory*, *3*(4), 393–414.

Meier, K. J., Pennington, M. S., & Eller, W. S. (2005). Race, sex, and Clarence Thomas: Representation change in the EEOC. *Public Administration Review*, *65*(2), 171–179.

Meier, K. J., & Stewart Jr., J. (1992). The impact of representative bureaucracies: Educational systems and public policies. *American Review of Public Administration*, *22*(3), 157–171.

Meier, K. J., Stewart, J., & England, R. E. (1989). *Race, class, and education: The politics of second-generation discrimination*. University of Wisconsin Press.

Meier, K. J., & Wilkins, V. M. (2002). Gender differences in agency head salaries: The case of public education. *Public Administration Review*, *62*(4), 405–411.

Meier, K. J., Wrinkle, R. D., & Polinard, J. L. (1999). Representative bureaucracy and distributional equity: Addressing the hard question. *Journal of Politics*, *61*(4), 1025–1039.

Mosher, F. C. (1968). *Democracy and the public service.* Oxford University Press.

Mosher, F. C. (1982). *Democracy and the public service.* Oxford University Press, USA.

Nicholson-Crotty, S., Nicholson-Crotty, J., & Fernandez, S. (2017). Will more black cops matter? Officer race and police-involved homicides of black citizens. *Public Administration Review, 77*(2), 206–216.

Nkomo, S. M. (1992). The emperor has no clothes: Rewriting race in organizations. *Academy of Management Reviews, 17*(3), 487–513.

Portillo, S., Bearfield, D., & Humphrey, N. (2020). The myth of bureaucratic neutrality: Institutionalized inequity in local government hiring. *Review of Public Personnel Administration, 40*(20), 516–531.

Riccucci, N. M., & Saidel, J. (1997). The representativeness of state-level bureaucratic leaders: A missing piece of the representative bureaucracy puzzle. *Public Administration Review, 57*(5), 423–430.

Riccucci, N. M., Van Ryzin, G. G., & Jackson, K. (2018). Representative bureaucracy, race, and policing: A survey experiment. *Journal of Public Administration Research and Theory, 28*(4), 506–518.

Roediger, David R. (2005). *Working toward whiteness: How America's immigrants became white.* Basic Books

Rosenbloom, D. H., & Featherstonhaugh, J. G. (1977). Passive and active representation in the federal service: A comparison of Blacks and Whites. *Social Science Quarterly, 57*(4), 873–882.

Rosette, A. S., Leonardelli, G. J., & Phillips, K. W. (2008). The White standard: Racial bias in leader categorization. *Journal of Applied Psychology, 93*(4), 758.

Sawyer, L. (2020). Ramsey County corrections officers of color say they were barred from guarding Derek Chauvin. Retrieved from: www.startribune.com/minority-corrections-officers-kept-from-monitoring-derek-chauvin-in-jail-george-floyd/571391442/.

Selden, S. C. (1997). Representative bureaucracy: Examining the linkage between passive and active representation in the farmers home administration. *The American Review of Public Administration, 27*(1), 22–42.

Skrentny, J. D. (2015). *After civil rights: Racial realism in the new American workplace.* Princeton University Press.

Sowa, J. E., & Selden, S. C. (2003). Administrative discretion and active representation: An expansion of the theory of representative bureaucracy. *Public Administration Review, 63*(6), 700–710.

Starke, A. M., Heckler, N., & Mackey, J. (2018). Administrative racism: Public administration education and race. *Journal of Public Affairs Education, 24*(4), 469–489.

Stivers, C. (2002). *Gender images in public administration: Legitimacy and the administrative state.* Sage Publications.

Stivers, C. (2007). "So poor and so black": Hurricane Katrina, public administration, and the issue of race. *Public Administration Review, 67*, 48–56.

Sy, T., Shore, L. M., Strauss, J., Shore, T. H., Tram, S., Whiteley, P., & Ikeda-Muromachi, K. (2010). Leadership perceptions as a function of race – Occupation fit: The case of Asian Americans. *Journal of Applied Psychology*, *95*(5), 902–919.

Thompson, S., & Hoggett, P. (1996). Universalism, selectivism and particularism: Towards a postmodern social policy. *Critical Social Policy*, *46*(16), 21–43.

Thompson, V. A. (1975). *Without sympathy or enthusiasm: The problem of administrative compassion*. University of Alabama Press.

Van Riper P.P. (1958). *History of the United States Civil Service*. Row and Peterson Press.

Waldo, D. (1974). Reflections on public morality. *Administration & Society*, *6*(3), 267–282.

Ward, J. (2008). White normativity: The cultural dimensions of whiteness in a racially diverse LGBT organization. *Sociological Perspectives*, *51*(3), 563–586.

Watkins-Hayes, C. (2011). Race, respect, and red tape: Inside the black box of racially representative bureaucracies. *Journal of Public Administration Research and Theory*, *21*(suppl 2), i233–i251.

Wilkins, V. M., & Keiser, L. R. (2006). Linking passive and active representation by gender: The case of child support agencies. *Journal of Public Administration Research and Theory*, *16*(1), 87–102.

Wise, L. R., & Tschirhart, M. (2000). Examining empirical evidence on diversity effects: how useful is diversity research for public-sector managers?. *Public Administration Review*, *60*(5), 386–394.

Witt, M. T. (2006). Notes from the margin: Race, relevance and the making of public administration. *Administrative Theory & Praxis*, *28*(1), 36–68.

5 The Myth of Legal Remedies

Kimberlé Crenshaw's earliest writings about intersectionality begin with a discussion of case law (1989). She is specifically focused on how the courts approached Title VII of the Civil Rights Act of 1964. Heralded as a significant shift in antidiscrimination law (Edelman, 2016), Title VII of the Civil Rights Act of 1964 prohibited employment discrimination based on race, sex, color, religion, or national origin. Three years later, the Age Discrimination in Employment Act was signed into law, providing additional age-based employment protections to those 40 years and older. Later, in 1990, the Americans with Disabilities Act passed, establishing another layer of employee protections for individuals with diagnosed disabilities.

While employment law has had a significant impact on public administration, it has not been the panacea that many believed it would be in the mid-twentieth century. Laws are not self-enforcing. Antidiscrimination law in the United States is enforced via regulation and litigation which often fall short of the ideals of equality. The lofty, but ambiguous, language of antidiscrimination law has led to complex, at times conflicting, court findings and complicated implementation strategies within public organizations. Ultimately, the law is one tool used to move public administration closer to equal outcomes and equitable processes, but the law alone is not enough.

The typical narrative of law as a remedy to social injustice in the United States focuses on blockbuster legislation and court cases, and the ways in which the Supreme Court affirms (or reaffirms) rights. We celebrate a number of these landmark cases, like *Brown v. Board of Education* (striking down school segregation) or *Obergefell v. Hodges* (establishing marriage equity). The basic idea is that the Supreme Court is confirming how these issues fit into our broader American ideals and the principles laid out in the Constitution. The narrative is presented as a linear progression, the Supreme Court leading a steady stream of cases

DOI: 10.4324/9781003322795-5

that move the country closer to our founding ideals. But, the role of law as a mechanism for social progress is much more complicated than that. Our purpose in this chapter is to explore the complicated social progression of the Courts through the myth of legal remedies. The myth of legal remedies is the idea that antidiscrimination law prevents, or at the very least remedies, racism, sexism, and other forms of discrimination within the modern workplace. The myth that there is a ready or easily accessible legal solution to workplace discrimination continues to permeate our field, but the history of the law and the accessibility of legal remedies is complicated.

Legal Progress in the United States

Contrary to popular belief, the law has not presented a linear progression of increased rights. The role of litigation generally, and the Supreme Court specifically, is more complicated than the prevailing narrative of courts enforcing rights. Some scholars assert there has never been a steady march toward more rights in the United States, but rather an unsteady march with civil rights gains only coming after significant internal and international pressure (Klinkner & Smith, 1999). These gains are often met with backlash or a re-entrenchment of the status quo. Klinkner and Smith (1999) assert that the law reflects this unsteady march, shifting with the broader socio-political climate. Ultimately, they argue that real civil rights gains are only achieved when America is held accountable in the broader global context. America cannot be seen as an international leader when rights are not being respected domestically. So, progress on racial equity largely comes when our society has a mirror held up on the global stage, typically while engaged in global conflict or war. This idea decenters the role of law in social progress and asserts that international politics shape domestic expectations and social movements.

Other scholars critique the classic legal narrative from a domestic perspective, pushing back against the idea that the Supreme Court has played a central role in affirming the core civil rights of Americans. Rosenberg (2008) argues that the Court does not create social progress. Rather, the Court is responding to social change that has already occurred in the United States and the Court is merely realigning the law to fit into social expectations of the culture of the day. When *Brown* was finally decided more than half of the states had already desegregated schools, and public opinion had turned against strict racial segregation in K-12 education. According to Rosenberg (2008), the Court confirms, but does not create social progress, and they only confirm progress because of pressure from the broader public.

A number of scholars have pushed back against Rosenberg's idea that Supreme Court rulings are not a significant part of the civil rights struggle, arguing that the law can be mobilized as one tool to push for social change, but it does not operate alone (McCann, 2006). McCann (2004) reframes the debate from whether the law (and legal cases) matter, to "how law does and does not matter." Ultimately, arguing that legal mobilization – using the law as a tool for social change – is complex and variable. He argues that many social movements rely on the push toward the Supreme Court to mobilize activists and other political actors. So, the Supreme Court alone does not make change, but they do inspire broader social movements. Without the Supreme Court and the promise of legal action, it would be hard to get individuals to invest their time or resources in social movements.

When specifically looking at law and affirmative action, Brown-Nagin (2005) argues that social movements advocating for equity and judicial law are fundamentally incompatible. The rhetoric around affirmative action is group oriented, advocating for progress for entire classes of people who have been historically marginalized in professional settings. However, each legal case is narrowly focused on a specific set of facts. While case law, and judicial decision-making, is narrowly focused, the goals of social movements are constructed as broad and inspirational. When it comes to workplace equity, legal decisions are not always aligned with advocates' goals (Brown-Nagin, 2005). Legal decisions are designed to provide relief to an individual, and often do not translate into structural change within workplaces or professions. Ultimately, the law is not an extension of social movements, but rather a tool that has been mobilized with variable success.

Crenshaw (1989) highlights the complications of relying on the law for social change in her exploration of three specific legal cases – *DeGraffenreid v. General Motors, Moore v. Hughes Helicopter*, and *Payne v. Travenol*. Each case seeks to provide clarity to Title VII of the Civil Rights Act of 1964. Across all of these cases, the Court approached the discussion of racial and gender discrimination in narrow ways, trying to fit the facts into their understanding of the antidiscrimination legislation. In each case, the Court ended up treating Black women differently, but never in a way that lived up to the lofty idealism often associated with the Civil Rights Act of 1964. In the *General Motors* case in particular, the Court refused to certify Black women as a class, noting that the law only provides protection for discrimination based on sex *or* race.

When looking across sex, white women masked the disparate outcomes Black women encountered with respect to their gender. When looking across race, Black men masked the disparate outcomes Black women encountered with respect to their race. The Courts found there was no legal remedy for Black women since they could not claim discrimination based on race *and* sex only race *or* sex. The Court held that their claim did not fit into the law, since Title VII says companies cannot discriminate based on race *or* sex. Crenshaw uses these cases as the basis to theorize about intersectionality as an approach to discussing identity, arguing that Black women face unique forms of oppression that cannot be understood as race plus gender, but must be understood as a unique experience of intersecting oppressions.

Our focus with this chapter is to explore limits of the law as a remedy for discrimination. We note that the law alone does not create social or organizational change, and having laws on the books that end discrimination does not necessarily mean we have no discrimination in practice. In each of the abovementioned court cases, Crenshaw discussed as the basis for her theory building, the Court tried to fit facts into the language of a statute and made divergent decisions, none of which concretely moved toward the abstract concept of antidiscrimination legislators presented. This meant that actions of employers, the practice in the real world, also did not fit into the lofty ideals of the legislation. Socio-legal scholars refer to this as the gap between the law on the books and law in practice (Calavita, 2016). While we may have laws that say what should happen, that does not necessarily mean that is what does happen.

In the next section, we explore how antidiscrimination law in the mid-twentieth century was held up as the solution to racial and gender injustice in the workplace, but the remedy has not been fully realized, leading to the myth of legal remedies in public organizations. Members of the public may believe that the laws in place mean discrimination does not happen, or if it does there are accessible remedies for it. We address that myth in this chapter. We first explore the rise of civil rights laws in the United States during the mid-twentieth century and focus on the promise of law as a remedy. We then dive into the critique of civil rights law and the myth of law as a complete remedy. Finally, we discuss the long shadow of the law as a mythical remedy for inequities in public organizations and how this shapes current workplace practices.

The Rise of Legal Remedies as a Foundation for Equity

The discussion of law and equal employment is typically broken into two main areas – equal employment opportunity (EEO) and affirmative action. EEO refers to laws and regulations aimed at ending discrimination in the workplace. EEO aims to ensure that individuals can get and retain jobs without current discrimination getting in the way, while affirmative action is focused on producing a more representative and diverse workforce. Affirmative action recognizes that past discrimination means modern workplaces do not accurately reflect our population, so affirmative action attempts to correct past injustice with a focus on corrective current day hires. Both EEO and affirmative action trace their origins to the mid-twentieth century. Scholars tend to refer to the mid-twentieth century as the Civil Rights Era, and they focus on legislation and judicial cases during this time as the foundation of modern decisions of civil rights law. However, the earliest civil rights legislation in our country was passed almost a century before that.

In this section, we will provide a brief overview of civil rights legislation and major court victories that serve as the foundation of EEO and affirmative action, before discussing the scholarly critique of legislation and judicial decision-making as remedies to discrimination. Throughout the chapter, we argue that law is an important tool in the fight to end discrimination in the workplace, but it is not the panacea that many had hoped it would be in the mid-twentieth century. Just because there are laws on the books saying that discrimination is illegal, does not mean that organizations or individuals abide by them. Laws themselves are not self-enforcing, but they do provide insight into how political leaders and policy makers understand the ideals of our country.

We can trace the origins of antidiscrimination law to the Reconstruction Era immediately following the Civil War. The 14th Amendment is one of three Reconstruction Amendments and formally required equal protection under the law. Although this amendment was added to the Constitution, legislation was also passed as part of early enforcement measures. The Civil Rights Act of 1866 focused mainly on property rights and guaranteeing property and contract rights for Black citizens. The main goal of this legislation was economic equity, ensuring that Black people could fully participate in American economic life. The Civil Rights Act of 1871 was also known as the Ku Klux Klan Act. This Act was designed as another enforcement measure for the 14th Amendment, directly addressing racial terrorism from the Ku Klux Klan and local government entities. The main goal of this legislation was to ensure that local governments did not interfere with new federal policies. It provided no new rights, but created policies to combat domestic terrorism used to prevent Black Americans from accessing their rights. While both of these Acts were largely ignored following the Reconstruction Era, section 1983 of the Civil Rights Act of 1871 became central to legal reforms in local governments in the mid-twentieth century. Section 1983 of the Civil Rights Act of 1871 allows individuals to sue local governments when those governments are failing to enforce equal rights. While these suits were routinely dismissed during the late nineteenth century, they saw significant success in the mid-twentieth century and are often credited for kicking off modern reforms in policing and law enforcement (for a review see Walker, 1998).

While the early civil rights legislation of the late-nineteenth century was largely ignored following reconstruction, the modern civil rights era of the twentieth century fared a bit better. It was during the mid-twentieth century that massive social movements related to racial justice led to a number of legal changes. Legislatively, the Civil Rights Act of 1964 made the most profound changes. The Civil Rights Act of 1964 was focused on discrimination within private employment. The passage of the Civil Rights Act of 1964 banned discrimination by private employers with more than 15 employees. Protections for public employees came eight years later with the EEO Act of 1972.

The marquee legislation of the Civil Rights Era was foundational to the shift in understanding of employment law and EEO. However, legislation and cases were not the only legal changes in the Civil Rights Era. Executive orders also played a role in demonstrating the centrality of employment law for the era. Specifically, executive orders which not only banned discrimination by government contractors, but also established quotas and other clear efforts to implement affirmative action to correct past discrimination in hiring. Both the passive laws against discrimination and the affirmative executive orders pushing for inclusion sparked significant legal cases that would extend into the twenty-first century trying to clarify exactly what political leaders meant and how reforms would shape the modern workplace.

While the profound legal progress of this era is undeniable, scholars and practitioners have been critical of many of the legal developments. Critiques focus on the legislation and judicial cases that followed as well as the cultural backlash to the Civil Rights Era. Below we discuss some of the main critiques of legal remedies for workplace inequities before discussing how the myth of legal remedies continues to shape current discussions of the modern workplace.

The Critique of Legal Remedies

One of the most significant critiques of civil rights legislation generally, and The Civil Rights Act of 1964 specifically, is ambiguity. Civil rights legislation focuses on big ideas and lofty goals, but does not always clearly state what success would look like or how to achieve that success. The Civil Rights Act of 1964 defines a number of terms and goals, but discrimination is not one of the terms defined. Edelman (2016) argues that this has led to two potentially competing interpretations of how the courts should understand the protections of the Civil Rights Act of 1964. There is a conservative interpretation that argues that the legislation is meant to promote color blind policies so each individual has opportunity regardless of their identities. Under this interpretation, antidiscrimination means removing all discussions of identity from the workplace and hiring decisions. There is a progressive interpretation that argues that the legislation was meant to address outcome-based equity and specific color and gender conscious policies that directly and explicitly corrected past discrimination based on identity groups. Under this interpretation, antidiscrimination work can only truly be done when confronting past discrimination and explicitly addressing how identity has been taken into account in the workplace and hiring decisions.

Both of these interpretations were discussed by legislators at the time, but the Civil Rights Act of 1964 passed without clear intent and with ambiguous language which has led to different interpretations and significantly different understandings of what we can rely on the legislation to provide. Historically, the executive branch has tended to focus on the progressive interpretation – encouraging affirmative policies to correct past wrongs including race and gender conscious remedies. This is a group-based approach that seeks to create and enforce policies that benefit entire communities. But, the courts have tended to favor the conservative interpretation, focusing on individual opportunities where organizations attempt to remove identity from decision-making processes. The courts prefer to focus on the specific facts of individual cases, without considering broader historical context. Rather than focusing on correcting historic injustices, the courts have focused on attempting to keep historical patterns and discussions of identity out of hiring decisions and workplace conflict.

Gotanda (1991) references this distinction in his discussion of "formal" race and "historical" race. Formal race references the social construction of race as a category, focusing on skin color and identity, but disconnected from historical context. Historical race acknowledges substance associated with categorization and recognizes that there are disadvantages associated with particular categories. Gotanda (1991) argues that some justices push for a particular kind of color blind constitutionalism, that only recognizes formal race, sees race as fixed (rather than contextualized to particular socio-political situations or positional), and something that should be removed from consideration whenever possible. Ultimately, Gotanda (1991) argues that nonrecognition, or removing race from consideration, is unrealistic. It is contradictory to say that race can be acknowledged as formal, but seen to have no influence on decision-making. The Court, however, took this approach in *City of Richmond v. J.A. Corson Co* (1989). In writing the majority opinion, Justice O'Connor argued that considering past racial discrimination in setting racial quotas for government contracting would move the country away from an explicit goal of a colorblind society. The Court held that any use of racial quotas for contracting should be held to strict scrutiny and indicated a clear preference for race-neutral policies. While many scholars have argued that race cannot be fully disentangled from personnel decisions within organizations or how the law is applied, the Justices firmly asserted a goal of removing consideration of race in personnel decision-making and focusing on individual decisions without historical or social context.

Since both the individual and group based approaches were discussed as part of the legislative process, it is unclear if one or the other approach truly had more support during the law's debate and passage. However, it is clear that the lack of clarity in the legislation that ultimately passed out of Congress and was signed by the President left the Courts in a difficult position and the law itself open to critique.

This ambiguity and lack of clear direction in the Civil Rights of 1964 has led many scholars to argue that workplace civil rights protections are symbolic and have not done enough to change the status quo of race and gender-based discrimination within modern American workplaces (Bumiller, 1992; Edelman, 2016; Berrey, Nelson, & Nielsen, 2017). Workplaces, however, are not passive in this symbolism. In fact, workplaces actively shape the court's expectations through a process Edelman (2016) describes as legal endogeneity.

At the heart of Edelman's (2016) argument about the limits of the law in the push for workplace equity is what she refers to as "symbolic structures." Symbolic structures are "a policy or procedure that is infused with value irrespective of its effectiveness. Symbolic structures connote attention to law or legal principles, whether or not they contribute to the substantive achievement of legal ideals" (p. 5). Saying that a policy or practice is symbolic does not mean that it is ineffective. Many symbolic structures have a substantive effect; however, that effect may not be as absolute as a court assumes. For example, many organizations have antidiscrimination language in their job postings. This language often claims that an organization is committed to inclusive hiring practices and does not discriminate. The organization may or may not have additional policies and practices in place to make the contents of this statement a reality. The statement may not be backed up by action, or even additional measures to assess the validity of the statement.

According to Edelman (2016), the courts often defer to organization's symbolic structures as evidence of a lack of discrimination. The courts see the statement as sufficient without considering implementation or measures of effectiveness. This judicial deference, where courts rely on an organization's formal policies, regardless of evidence of effectiveness, leads to legal endogeneity. Legal endogeneity arguments upend traditional thinking about the law. The traditional idea is that law is created by policy makers and implemented by organizations and workers. However, the theory of legal endogeneity posits that organizations create policies and programs to symbolize response to the law, law that is often ambiguous in what it is requiring of organizations. As these symbolic policies and practices become commonplace within a field, courts, other organizations, and even employees begin to equate the symbolic response to ambiguous law to actual legal responses. Legal compliance is seen as synonymous with adoption of prevalent policies and practices, regardless of effectiveness.

The courts rely on organizations to formalize ambiguous antidiscrimination legislation through their own policies and practices. Deference to these policies and practices by the courts means that organizations, more so than policy makers, are truly defining what it means to adhere to antidiscrimination legislation. Organizations have an incentive to respond in symbolic, rather than substantive ways, because it is less disruptive and more cost-effective and efficient for them. Ultimately, the judicial deference to symbolic structures in organizations reinforces the status quo, where society accepts a lack of action to combat ongoing and persistent structural discrimination against people of color, women, and queer and transgender people within the workplace.

While Edelman (2016) considers how organizations respond to the law, a number of other scholars consider how individuals who mobilize the law to combat discrimination fare. These scholars explore the experience of the individual rather than the organization. Individuals who experience discrimination must first decide if they will engage with the law as a tool, and if they do mobilize the law in their effort to combat discrimination it does not always work out.

Bumiller (1992) centers victims of discrimination in her scholarship, often finding that they do not engage with the law as a potential remedy to discrimination because of high social costs. There is an underlying assumption in much of the legal scholarship that if people know about their legal rights, they will mobilize their rights through legal action. However, Bumiller (1992) argues that "much of what has been written about civil rights policies is based on the exceptional cases that reach appellate courts, rather than on cases where individuals have experienced discrimination and have not fought it" (p. 2). She pushes back against the mainstream assumption that if people know about the law they will use it, arguing that people often do not mobilize the law because it would come at a high social cost to them through their own understanding of themselves and/or disrupted relationships.

People who have experienced discrimination must first identify as victims before engaging the law as a potential remedy. They have to muster resources to engage with a lawyer to take on their case. Engaging with the law as a potential remedy severs social connections and can put employment and personal relationships in jeopardy. For instance, several studies have found that women are unlikely to report sex-based discrimination for fear of retaliation (Rubin & Alteri, 2019; Yu & Lee, 2019). Many people choose not to engage with the law as a potential remedy because of the personal risks and costs that come with filing a legal claim. In this case, knowledge of the law does not necessarily mean that people have power in a situation. Invoking the law may only disrupt their lives and livelihood without much of a chance for true relief. Filing a legal claim is often about more than winning or losing the individual claim, it has the ability to disrupt the workplace and multiple social relationships.

While Bumiller (1992) considers why people may not want to mobilize the law in response to discrimination, Berrey et al. (2017) explore what happens when they do. They argue that we see a paradox in employment civil rights law. There is a significant normative commitment to employment rights law as evidenced by the rise of employment rights professionals in a number of workplaces, as well as increasing trainings on how to file discrimination claims. However, there is also a significant legal re-entrenchment of traditional power structures with increasingly narrow rulings on civil rights claims and significant outcry against civil rights litigation as frivolous, costly, and misguided. Berrey et al. (2017) complete extensive empirical analysis of filed employment discrimination claims. They find that:

> although antidiscrimination law holds employers legally accountable by forbidding workplace discrimination, we find that the system of employment civil rights litigation is substantially controlled by employers ... such deference is part of the broader phenomenon of *reinscription*.... the process by which the ascriptive hierarchies that the law is intended to disrupt are reified and rearticulated through law in the workplace and court.
>
> (emphasis in original, p. 11)

They build on Edelman's (2016) earlier argument that employers themselves do so much to shape how antidiscrimination law is understood that it almost becomes useless for employees who claim discrimination. Their analysis goes further than Edelman (2006) with an in-depth empirical exploration of how individuals' cases fare.

After the Civil Rights Act of 1964 was expanded with the Equal Employment Opportunity Act of 1972, there was a steady uptick in discrimination cases filed with the EEO Commission and in courts. Discrimination cases saw a steady increase throughout the 1980s and 1990s; however, that trend has not continued into the twenty-first century (Berrey et al., 2017). Additionally, while there is a cultural focus on big class action lawsuits, involving multiple plaintiffs in a large company, the vast majority of antidiscrimination cases are filed by single plaintiffs putting an individual case forward. Individual, rather than class action suits have increasingly become the norm as the number of overall cases has dwindled. Some of this shift from class action lawsuits, and the decline in the number of overall suits, may be due in part to Supreme Court rulings in the 1980s and 1990s that limited how and which cases may move forward by narrowing the focus of lawsuits and setting more stringent procedural standards. The Court throughout the 1990s made it more difficult for employees to form classes and initiate class action suits. "In fact, the estimated probability of a proclass action outcome dropped from 59% in the late 1980s to 26% in 2013" (Berrey et al., 2017, p. 37). The Court also shifted from a focus on impact to intent in discrimination filings. Specifically, in *Wards Cove v. Antonio* (1989) the Court held that demonstrating disparate impact is not enough, claimants must demonstrate that disparities are a result of specific practices of the employer. Meaning it was harder for employees to mobilize the law collectively and they must attempt to prove that employer's actions were intentional, rather than just demonstrate disparate impacts based on race, sex, or other protected classes.

Like Bumiller (1992), Berrey et al. (2017) argue that not all discrimination results in legal filings. They take this a step further though exploring filings moving from Equal Employment Opportunity Commission (EEOC) claims to litigation. They find that contrary to popular narratives, the vast majority of legal claims do not see success in court and very few legal claims result in monetary payouts. Looking at a random sample of discrimination cases filed between 1988 and 2003, Berrey et al. (2017) find that class action suits make up less than one percent of cases. A key indicator of success for cases is the presence of legal representation, when a plaintiff does not have an attorney there is a 40 percent chance that their case is almost immediately thrown out. This means that there is a resource element at play for who has access to move forward with an antidiscrimination claim. When plaintiffs do not have ready or easy access to attorneys, they are less likely to be able to mobilize their rights. Even when a case moves forward, the vast majority settle for a modest amount of money rather than going to trial. Settlements typically mean that employers do not admit fault. Contrary to media portrayals or popular myths of plaintiffs winning massive payouts, most discrimination claims are summarily dismissed or result in minor settlements that do not include findings of fault against employers.

As Bumiller (1992) points out, mobilizing the law is disruptive to the individual lives and relationships of people facing discrimination. But, Berrey et al. (2017) further argue that the disruption typically does not result in a worthwhile payout. In fact, the legal system does not fully hear most claims (dismissing them early in the process) and rarely finds for the plaintiff in the discrimination cases. But, the myth of legal remedies continues to permeate the field. In the next section, we will discuss the long shadow of legal remedies as a solution to discrimination and how this myth continues to shape public administration.

The Long Shadow of Legal Remedies as Solution to Overt and Subtle Discrimination

Many of us have heard a classmate, colleague, acquaintance, or friend say, "but, that's illegal" in response to someone sharing their experience of discrimination in the workplace or at school. When we teach about antidiscrimination law, many of our students want to believe that the legal battles of the mid- and late-twentieth century have solved the problems of overt and subtle discrimination. But movements like #MeToo demonstrate that legal battles won in the twentieth century have not completely eliminated discrimination in the twenty-first century. #MeToo was a phrase initially used in 2006 by Tarana Burke on social media to call attention to the frequency and normalcy of sexual harassment. The #MeToo movement, and similar movements since, has continued to demonstrate the frequency and prevalence of discrimination within workplace settings and public organizations. This is not meant to diminish the monumental progress of legal battles in the twentieth century, but we must acknowledge that laws alone will not address the systemic racism, sexism, homophobia, and transphobia in our communities and workplaces.

The myth of legal remedies in the United States context relies on the broad narrative of rights in our country. The idea that we all have rights that are equally valued, affirmed in organizations we work in and the communities we live in, and are self-enforcing. As Berrey et al. (2017) note:

> Rights are a significant source of power because we construe them to (at least formally) be available equally to everyone, neutral, and backed by the legitimate authority of the state. When rights are vindicated in courts, social actors are expected to take notice and implement changes (for example, in workplace policies) to achieve social change.
>
> (p. 12)

However, rights are not self-enforcing and are necessarily shaped and implemented based on the broader political context. For generations, scholars have explored the mobilization of rights and the gap between laws on the books discussing rights and how rights are enforced or understood by government actors and the courts (Calavita, 2016; Epp, 2010; McCann, 2006). When rights aren't respected, they are not always mobilized via courts or in formal processes. The rhetoric of rights, or just discussing rights, can also shape expectations of individuals and organizations.

Some scholars point to extra-judicial rights enforcement via "legalized accountability" in bureaucratic settings as one way that the broader narrative of rights and rights rhetoric shape public organizations, even in the absence of legal victories (Epp, 2010; Edelman, 2016). With a legalized accountability framework, public administrators will often point to the threat of litigation or the potential of legal sanction as a reason to make organizational reforms. While we saw from the last section that successful litigation as an enforcement mechanism for workplace rights may be rare, the perceived threat of litigation may be enough to push some organizational actors to act in ways that respect rights and reform workplace cultures to support workers' rights.

Similarly, Engel and Munger (2003) discuss how the rhetoric of rights shapes individuals' perceptions of what they can expect from organizations. They analyze in-depth interviews with people with disabilities about the passage and implementation of the Americans with Disabilities Act (1990). They find that just the passage of the Americans with Disabilities Act, and subsequent conversations about it, shape individual's expectations, even if they have not formally mobilized the law for an accommodation. They argue that legal consciousnesses, in the form of rights consciousness, shape how individuals engage with organizations. The law can shape the behavior of individuals and organizations even when it is not formally invoked.

However, just because the law can shape expectations and behavior does not mean that it always does. As scholars have noted for generations through empirical and theoretical work, informal and formal mechanisms of legal enforcement tend to favor those with social, financial, and political power (Galanter, 1974; Miller & Sarat, 1980; Berrey et al., 2017). Informal and formal processes of rights mobilization have been criticized since they require individuals who have been marginalized or discriminated against to use a "victim" framework (Bumiller, 1992), and continue to frame discrimination as an interpersonal issue rather than a systemic one (Lucas, 2009). It is likely not possible to end discrimination through individual legal cases or based on the passage of single pieces of legislation. The myth of legal remedies remains strong in public administration. Rights and the law matter, but they are not enough on their own to end discrimination in our field or in the workplace.

Conclusion

The law is a powerful tool for social progress and social change. However, the law is not self-enforcing and must be understood and implemented by courts and organizations. Significant legal progress was made in the mid-twentieth century during the Civil Rights Era, but that progress has not led to the elimination of workplace discrimination or a uniform understanding of how the law should operate. As part of the myth of legal remedies, there is an attempt to provide a simplistic narrative of how reform happens in the United States – a steady march towards enacting the ideals of our founding. However, scholars have found time and time again that there is no steady march. The implementation of the law is more complicated than a simplistic narrative of progress. That does not mean the law is not important, but alone cannot rid us of inequities.

In the next chapter, we move away from discussing the myths of the field and toward a new framework for how to address inequities in public administration scholarship and practice. By using a historically grounded positionality framework, we can dismantle the myths of the field and concretely address how identity is understood and evolves within our field. The historically grounded positionality framework gives us another ways to understand and address longstanding structural inequalities.

Works Cited

Cases

Brown v. Board of Education, 347 U.S. 483 (1954).
City of Richmond v. J.A. Corson Co, 488 U.S. 469 (1989).
DeGraffenreid v. GENERAL MOTORS ASSEMBLY DIV., ETC., 413 F. Supp. 142 (E.D. Mo. 1976).
Moore v. Hughes Helicopters, Inc., 708 F.2d 475 (9th Cir. 1983).
Obergefell v. Hodges, 576 U.S. 644 (2015).
Payne v. Travenol Laboratories, Inc., 673 F.2d 798 (5th Cir. 1982).
Wards Cove Packing Co. v. Antonio, 490 US 642 (1989).

Legislation

Americans with Disabilities Act of 1990, Pub. L. No. 101-336, 104 Stat. 328 (1990).
Civil Rights Act of 1964 § 7, 42 U.S.C. §2000e et seq (1964).

Literature

Berrey, E., Nelson, R. L., & Nielsen, L. B. (2017). *Rights on trial: How workplace discrimination law perpetuates inequality*. University of Chicago Press.
Brown-Nagin, T. (2005). Elites, social movements, and the law: The case of affirmative action. *Columbia Law Review, 105*, 1436.
Bumiller, K. (1992). *The civil rights society: The social construction of victims*. Johns Hopkins University Press.
Calavita, K. (2016). *Invitation to law and society: An introduction to the study of real law*. University of Chicago Press.
Crenshaw, K. (1989). Demarginalizing the intersection of race and sex: A black feminist critique of antidiscrimination doctrine, feminist theory and anti-racist politics. *University of Chicago Legal Forum*, 139–168.
Edelman, L. B. (2016). *Working law*. University of Chicago Press.
Engel, D. M., & Munger, F. W. (2003). *Rights of inclusion*. University of Chicago Press.
Epp, C. R. (2010). *Making rights real*. University of Chicago Press.
Galanter, M. (1974). Why the haves come out ahead: Speculations on the limits of legal change. *Law & Society Review, 9*, 95.
Gotanda, N. (1991). A critique of "our constitution is color-blind". *Stanford Law Review, 44*, 1–68.
Klinkner, P. A., & Smith, R. M. (1999). *The unsteady march: The rise and decline of racial equality in America*. University of Chicago Press.
Lucas, S. (2009). *Theorizing discrimination in an era of contested prejudice: Discrimination in the United States*. Temple University Press.

McCann, M. (2006). Law and social movements: Contemporary perspectives. *Annual Review of Law and Social Science, 2*, 17–38.

McCann, M. W. (2004). Law and social movements. In A. Sarat (Ed.), *The Blackwell companion to law and society* (pp. 506–522). Blackwell/Dartmouth.

Miller, R. E., & Sarat, A. (1980). Grievances, claims, and disputes: Assessing the adversary culture. *Law and Society Review, 15*(3/4), 525–566.

Rosenberg, G. N. (2008). *The hollow hope*. University of Chicago Press.

Rubin, E. V., & Alteri, A. M. (2019). Discrimination complaints in the U.S. federal government: Reviewing progress under the No FEAR Act. *Review of Public Personnel Administration, 39*(4), 511–522.

Walker, S. (1998). *The rights revolution: Rights and community in modern America*. Oxford University Press on Demand.

Yu, H. H., & Lee, D. (2019). Women and public organization: An examination of mentorship and its effect on reporting workplace discrimination. *Review of Public Personnel Administration, 41*(2), 274–293.

6   Moving from Myth to Reality

The standard narrative of the origin of American Public Administration as a field starts with a discussion of the Progressive Era. The typical story argues that the field started as a response to rampant political corruption in the late-nineteenth and early-twentieth centuries. The response to political corruption was a focus on technical skill and a decoupling of the administrative, technocratic aspects of government from politics. The first great innovation of the field was the politics-administration dichotomy. The idea that the administration and implementation of policies should be devoid of politics was introduced by Woodrow Wilson as part of his argument that public administration is a stand-alone field, distinct from politics, law, or economics (1887/2007). The standard way this is discussed is that elected leaders should make policies and set the agenda and direction for governments at all levels – local, state, and federal – but skilled technocrats should carry out these policies, ensuring that they are implemented in the most effective and efficient way possible. Proponents argued that this approach would not only remove the political corruption of the time, but would also allow science to serve as the foundation for management for policy implementation – leading to increases in government efficiency and effectiveness.

Within a few decades, scholars decisively pushed back against the core of this origin story noting that there is no clear politics-administration dichotomy (Fesler, 1957). That even the smallest decisions regarding implementation have political consequences (Waldo, 1948). The standard story of the field is that we grew out of this initial origin story of public administration to understand that administration and policy implementation are more complicated and nuanced than our founders initially thought. Early critiques focused on the more nuanced and complicated relationship between politics and administration. As the twentieth century progressed, so did our sophistication with regard to management practices. By the Civil Rights Era, scholars of the field

DOI: 10.4324/9781003322795-6

started to understand that administrators have a central role in ensuring that governments at all levels (local, state, and federal) implement policies and practices and ensure not just effectiveness and efficiency, but also equity. One of the central contributions of public administration scholars during the Civil Rights Era was the addition of social equity as a third pillar of the field (Gooden & Portillo, 2011). During this period, Frederickson (2015) asked the important question, efficiency and effectiveness for whom, acknowledging that the identities of constituents have mattered throughout our history when it comes to service and outcomes in public administration.

Though even as the field moved toward a more nuanced understanding of the relationship between politics and administration and an understanding of the importance of social equity, the critiques of the mid-twentieth century rarely discussed the ways that race or xenophobia played a role in the early insistence on public administration decoupled from politics. Much of this decoupling of administration and politics was happening as Black people and newly arrived immigrants were gaining political power. There was little discussion of how the founding of the field had institutionalized an understanding of administration as neutral, even though scholars were realizing that it was far from neutral. The idea of a neutral bureaucracy, devoid of politics, had become taken for granted within the scholarship and practice of public administration what Meyer and Rowan (1977) would term a rationalized myth. A rationalized myth is an idea so taken for granted it has become decoupled from its original source. Even with the focus on equity during the Civil Rights Era, there was still little interrogation of how the structures and practices of the field had been shaped by earlier eras. As scholars and practitioners today are continuing to push for equity within the field, a historically grounded positionality framework can help us take into account the ways that the past continues to shape our work.

These ongoing discussions about the origins of the field demonstrate that our history is not settled. This standard origin story of our field leaves out key perspectives. It establishes a number of myths that continue to dominate our field, regardless of the evidence of their faulty or incomplete foundations. Throughout this book we have presented some of the core myths this origin story generates – the myth of neutrality, the myth of merit, and the myth of representation. These are not necessarily the only myths present in our field, but they each demonstrate how we need to do a more thorough job of interrogating our history and recognizing how it continues to contribute to our present scholarship and practice. In this chapter, we discuss the ways that the myths of our field continue to influence our work today and present the historically grounded positionality framework. This framework provides a way to take the past into account as we continue to improve the work of the modern administrative state.

The Past in the Present

There are some very public approaches to wrestling with the past that are playing out recently. Woodrow Wilson was once largely heralded as one of the founding scholars of the field, but his reputation has shifted significantly in recent years. His name was removed from the School of Public Affairs at Princeton in 2020. He served as President of the University before winning the U.S. Presidential election in 1912. When removing Wilson's name, the current University President stated, "racist thinking and policies make him an inappropriate namesake for a school or college whose scholars, students and alumni must stand firmly against racism in all its forms" (Pietsch, 2020). Princeton President Christopher Eisgruber went on to say that Wilson's policies regarding segregation in government service led him to be an inappropriate name sake.

Wilson was elected U.S. President in 1912, and quickly moved to segregate the federal civil service (Yellin, 2013). Though, as Yellin (2013) points out, Wilson did not act alone in his push for segregated public service. What was unique about this time period, was the efforts of the Wilson administration *and* Progressive reformers to marry the ideas of a segregated civil service and progressive politics. These reforms resulted in the loss of significant political power of the Black middle class and Black civil servants. In more modern times, the reforms have been discussed as a reaction to patronage and political corruption, and that was certainly part of the reform efforts. But, another aspect, with lasting consequences was the segregation of the civil service and the institutionalization of white supremacy in public service. The removal of Black civil servants from positions of power during the Wilson presidency happened alongside the growth of the administrative state. Once Black civil servants were removed from their positions, whiteness became normalized within these spaces and just a few years later these very racialized decisions were presented and remembered as based on meritocratic principles of administration based on effectiveness. The role of Black civil servants in the Reconstruction Era is rarely discussed in the field, particularly as part of the origin of the growth of the administrative state and focus on efficiency within government service. This more complex origin of the field provides an important foundation as we move beyond the origin myths of our field.

Even though the politics-administration dichotomy has been critiqued for more than half a century, scholars still regularly revisit debates around it (McCandless & Guy, 2013). McCandless and Guy (2013) argue that the field has multiple definitions of the politics-administration dichotomy that all ultimately try to distinguish the boundary between politics and administration. These various definitions – ranging from a full separation to a separation of partisan politics to a simple theoretical heuristic – vary because of a lack of shared understanding of the field's history and Wilson's original argument. They assert that there must be a shared understanding of our history and revisit Wilson's writings to argue that Wilson did not intend for a dichotomy, but rather a distinction.

A distinction would establish the field as unique from other fields, providing boundaries and focus. They argue that criticism of the dichotomy often rests on understanding it as absolute, but this was not necessarily the original intention. Even as scholars have now regularly noted that the politics-administration dichotomy was likely not meant to be an absolute (Svara, 1998; McCandless & Guy, 2013), it is still a regularly employed heuristic that is often taken on face value and presented as foundational to our field. Answering McCandless and Guy's (2013) call for a shared understanding of our history does not necessarily mean that we must reject the founding, but it does mean that we have to develop a more nuanced understanding of it. One of the significant aspects that we rarely discuss within public administration is the racialized and gendered nature of the field's origins and how that continues to today.

The Role of Identity in Public Administration

The myths of our field have consistently assumed a default white masculine heteronormative identity. As we discussed in Chapter 2, our understandings of identity have become more sophisticated, but we still have work to do to understand that identity is not a static concept. While public administration scholars are increasingly using feminist, intersectional, and queer frameworks to understand identity (see Breslin, Pandey, & Riccucci, 2017 for a review), our work regularly falls short of fully realizing the complexities of identity in public organizations.

How people interpret and perform their identities is constantly evolving. How identity is understood by individuals, organizations, and cultures changes over time. Looking specifically at gender, when public administration was established as a field, many thought of gender as two binary categories associated with biological characteristics. However, we now know that gender refers to a range of socially constructed characteristics that fall along, and may fluidly move between feminity and masculinity. While individuals may identify with a completely feminine or masculine understandings of their own gender, they may also fall somewhere between these binaries or move fluidly between them. This evolving understanding of gender has led many public organizations to change the way they collect demographic data about employees and clients, shaped how we discuss issues of gender within the workplace, and influenced discussions of who can or should be a public administrator and how public administrators should serve their communities. Similarly, how the public and professionals understand race, ethnicity, ability, sexual orientation, and a number of other identities has evolved over time. This evolution affects the workplace of public administration as well as the communities we serve.

Historically grounded positionality acknowledges that understandings of identity evolve over time, and how we as a society have historically viewed race, ethnicity, gender, sexual orientation, and other identities continues to shape policies and practices within public organizations today. The historically grounded positionality framework gives us a way to discuss modern inequities in context, and a framework for discussing how we move forward with addressing inequities in public administration. It helps us to understand changes in the field of practice of public administration – who is a public administrator and how do we create more inclusive organizations – as well as the communities we serve – how can we deliver efficient, effective, and truly equitable services.

Our approach builds on traditions of positionality from feminist scholarship and incorporates intersectionality, while also acknowledging that geographic and temporal nuances shape how individuals and communities understand identity (Anthias, 2002; Doan & Portillo, 2017, 2019). Understandings of identity have evolved over our nation's and our field's history. Ultimately, we argue that identity is positional – dependent on the institutions and communities an individual engages with. The discussion above provides a terrific example of this. During Reconstruction, a number of Black civil servants worked their way into and up in the federal bureaucracy. But, during the Progressive Era the federal civil service became segregated. Black civil servants did not suddenly become less qualified, but society's understanding of their identity shifted as the politics around them shifted (King, 1995). Modern discussions of identity continue to shift. Current discussions around diversity in the workplace argue that having people with a variety of lived experiences and social identities may make organizations stronger. Diversity in leadership and workforces has been linked to better outcomes in organizations and more legitimacy because the organizations reflect the communities they serve (Riccucci, 2021).

However, these discussions of identity focus on the organization level rather than the individual, noting that identity happens in relation to others within the organization. Benefits focus on organizational outcomes and the ways that organizations are more than individual hiring decisions. Modern approaches to discussing diversity in the workplace often acknowledge the benefits of diverse workforces, but may also reinforce a racialized and gendered essentialism that fails to take positionality into account. Meaning that focusing on what diverse perspectives bring to organizations may not thoroughly acknowledge how individuals experience their identities and how they are treated within the workplace. Through the lens of our historically grounded positionality approach, we can consider the individual and organization within context. The myth of neutrality quickly falls apart. Instead, what emerges is a distorted picture of merit and representation that continues to shape the way we think about public administration today. By engaging with public administration scholarship and practice with a historically grounded positionality approach, we demonstrate how the field can move towards a more equitable administrative state.

Historically Grounded Positionality

Discussions of identity abound in the social sciences. We discussed a number of theoretical frameworks and scholarly traditions of identity in Chapter 2. In particular, we focused on the ways that public administration scholarship has increasingly understood how identity shapes the experiences of people working within organizations as well as people receiving services. There are a number of dimensions that we can discuss when it comes to identity – race, gender, and sexual orientation are the three that we have focused on throughout this book. However, identity is not a single dimension for any individual. Throughout this book, we have discussed the ways that intersectionality, growing out of Kimberle Crenshaw's (1989) critical legal scholarship, provides a framework to understand the ways that multiple oppressions shape the experiences of individuals. Briefly, Crenshaw (1989) argues that the experiences of Black women are not simply the addition of race plus gender, but that these two structures intersect to create unique experiences that cannot be understood as simply additive. She uses legal cases to explore how the law in the United States is not written in a way to fully encapsulate the experience of Black women, and that all women or all Black people cannot serve as reliable stand ins for this experience (see Chapters 2 and 5 for a more complete discussion).

While intersectionality has provided a more nuanced way to understand how multiple oppressions operate within a social context, it has been criticized as a static view of identity (Anthias, 2002; Bose, 2012; Doan & Portillo, 2017; Nash, 2008). In particular, scholars doing research in transnational contexts argued that there is an inattentiveness to spatial and temporal contexts in many studies using an intersectional framework. Scholars working with migrant populations argued that social positions fluctuate within and between national contexts with accordance to location (Ahmed, 2011; Purkayastha, 2010). The contextual nature of identity may also put an individual's internalized expectations of their own identity in contrast with ascribed understandings of their identity. For example, a Black American woman working in India may have an internalized understanding of her identities as marginalized or othered because of the oppression she experiences in the United States; however, when abroad, the privilege of her citizenship positions her differently within context. Further understandings of identity are wholly dependent on the relational context between individuals within an interaction. When a Latina woman is interacting with a white peer in the workplace there is a different social hierarchy and dynamic at play than when that same woman is interacting with a Black non-binary peer in a social context. "Conceptually and in practice, identity is situational and fluid. It changes depending on where a person is geographically located and with whom they are interacting at a particular time" (Doan & Portillo, 2017, p. 238). This positional understanding of identity (England, 1994) grows out of feminist methodologies that center interactions. Identity is not something that is static to an individual, but happens within interactions and social constructs. This means that identity is not just individual, but also contextual and cultural. An individual understands their identity within a larger cultural unit like an organization or community. That individual's identity is also understood and reinforced by the other members of that cultural unit. Identity is not something that happens alone, but between people, reinforced with interactions.

We take the traditional feminist understandings of positionality a step further, arguing that identity is shaped by historical positioning as well as modern understandings. As we discussed in Chapter 2, the field's understanding of neutrality was originally racialized and gendered. While that history may not be front of mind for most individuals as they go about their work, it continues to shape how individuals understand and operationalize views of identity in the workplace.

The decontextualization of the practice of public administration has allowed the myth of bureaucratic neutrality to thrive. We argue that by intentionally considering how the past shapes understandings of identity and the inequities of the present, we can encourage more nuanced conversations around social equity and move the field forward towards more equity centered practices.

Historically grounded positionality is a framework for understanding that the past shapes the present and the current position from which we view the world. Societal views of identity and equity change over time. For example, even the understanding of who is included and excluded in the racial category of white has changed. Some of the immigrants reformers rallied against as othered during the Progressive Era – Italians and Eastern Europeans – are now understood as white in the U.S. context (Barrett & Roediger, 2005; Guglielmo & Salerno, 2012). As Jim Crow laws were put in place following the Progressive Era, there was an increasing race consciousness among older (typically Western European) and newer (typically Southern and Eastern) European immigrants. During the Progressive Era, newer immigrants were often excluded from the racial category of white. But, part of the Americanization of these newer immigrants was also an expansion of the racial category of white to include them and define them in contrast to Black Americans. Our identities are shaped and understood by history, context, relationships, and community; different identity groups (and individuals within them) may have different levels of awareness of the historical context that informs the present. To move forward we must work to understand history, how our own identities were shaped, and how our communities understand identity and belonging. We are often unaware of how these types of policy histories shape our understanding of current inequities in the modern day workplace. These histories contribute to the subtle and overt stereotypes that often shape our understanding of who belongs in the workplace, who is seen as a leader, and who is seen as most competent.

This is something that affects the individual, organizational, and community level of our work. At the individual level, this shows up as how individuals understand their own identity and how their identity shapes their experiences in the workplace or as clients of bureaucracies. Within the field, we may study this by considering how identity shapes work experiences (do women and men experience differences in salaries or job satisfaction; do clients of color have different outcomes than white clients). This also shapes our work at the organizational level. How function may differ based on historic practices related to gender, race, and sexual orientation. There are stereotypes of what a leader looks like or what kind of family arrangement they have that may shape hiring decisions and expectations throughout the organization. Organizations may have particular practices that are shaped by histories or identities that are taken for granted by the workforce.

The earliest discussions of identity within our field focused on communities and the people we serve. As scholars developed social equity as a pillar of the field, it was outward facing, considering effectiveness and efficiency for whom (Gooden & Portillo, 2011; Frederickson, 1980). Considering the identity make up of communities is incredibly important and knowing that professional administrators are making decisions that ensure equity within the field is core to the ethical performance of our work. In public administration, we regularly discuss the outcomes for communities we serve, but the ways in which this impacts public administrators is also important. We have to be able to discuss communities served while also considering who is serving those communities. Considering the identities of communities and public administrators and how those identities were shaped is key to breaking down the myths of public administration. As we move forward in this work, we should consider the cultural and historical context of our work.

Conclusion

Identity is more than a single dimension. As theoretical frameworks around identity have become more nuanced, scholars present a better understanding of individuals and their organizations and communities. Individual's identities are best understood positionally, within context to other individuals, organizations, and communities. A feminist positional and intersectional understanding of identity still needs further expansion to include a strong understanding of how histories shape identities for individuals and communities. A historically grounded positionality framework insists that we understand how the past shapes the present.

In the next chapter, we focus on how the historically grounded positionality framework can be used to dismantle the myth of neutrality in public administration. By critically examining our past, we develop a more nuanced understanding regarding how inequities operate in public administration today. By critically examining our past, we also break down the myths that have been a part of our field for decades. Once we move past these myths and have a better understanding of how public administration functions within the U.S. context, we can make better decisions for our future.

94   *Moving from Myth to Reality*

Works Cited

Ahmed, A. (2011). Belonging out of context: The intersection of place, networks and ethnic identity among retired British migrants living in the Costa Blanca. *Journal of Identity and Migration Studies, 5*(2), 2–19.

Anthias, F. (2002). Where do I belong? Narrating collective identity and translocational positionality. *Ethnicities, 2*(4), 491–514.

———. (2008). Thinking through the lens of translocational positionality: An intersectionality frame for understanding identity and belonging. *Translocations: Migration and Social Change, 4*(1), 5–20. Retrieved from http://hdl.handle.net/10552/3331.

———. (2012). Transnational mobilities, migration research and intersectionality. *Nordic Journal of Migration Research, 2*(2), 102–110. doi:10.2478/v10202-011-0032-y.

Barrett, J. E., & Roediger, D. (2005). How white people became white. In P. S. Rothenberg (Ed.), *White privilege: Essential readings on the other side of racism* (pp. 29–34). Worth Publishers.

Bearfield, D. A. (2009). Equity at the intersection: Public administration and the study of gender. *Public Administration Review, 69*(3), 383–386.

Blessett, B. (2018). Symposium on cultural competence, accountability, and social justice: Administrative responsibility and the legitimacy of United States democracy. *Public Integrity, 20*(4), 321–324.

Bose, C. E. (2012). Intersectionality and global gender inequality. *Gender & Society, 26*(1), 67–72. doi:10.1177/0891243211426722.

Breslin, R. A., Pandey, S., & Riccucci, N. M. (2017). Intersectionality in public leadership research: A review and future research agenda. *Review of Public Personnel Administration, 37*(2), 160–182.

Crenshaw, K. (1989). Demarginalizing the intersection of race and sex: A black feminist critique of antidiscrimination doctrine, feminist theory and anti-racist politics. *University of Chicago Legal Forum,* 139–168.

Doan, A. & Portillo, S. (2017). Not a woman, but a soldier: Exploring identity through translocational positionality. *Sex Roles, 76,* 236–249.

Doan, A., & Portillo, S. (2019). *Organizational obliviousness: Entrenched resistance to gender integration in the military*. Cambridge University Press.

England, K. V. (1994). Getting personal: Reflexivity, positionality, and feminist research. *The Professional Geographer, 46*(1), 80–89.

Fesler, J. W. (1957). Administrative literature and the second hoover commission reports. *American Political Science Review, 51*(1), 135–157.

Frederickson, H. G. (1980). *New public administration*. University Alabama Press.

Frederickson, H. G. (2015). *Social equity and public administration: Origins, developments, and applications*. Routledge.

Gaynor, T. S., & Blessett, B. (2014). Inequality at the intersection of the Defense of Marriage Act and the Voting Rights Act: A review of the 2013 Supreme Court decisions. *Administrative Theory & Praxis, 36*(2), 261–267.

Gooden, S., & Portillo, S. (2011). Advancing social equity in the Minnowbrook tradition. *Journal of Public Administration Research and Theory*, *21*(suppl_1), i61–i76.

Guglielmo, J., & Salerno, S. (Eds.). (2012). *Are Italians white? How race is made in America*. Routledge.

King, D. (1995). *Separate and unequal: Black Americans and the U.S. federal government*. Oxford University Press.

McCandless, S. A., & Guy, M. E. (2013). One more time: What did Woodrow Wilson really mean about politics and administration? *Administrative Theory & Praxis*, *35*(3), 356–377.

Meyer, J. W., & Rowan, B. (1977). Institutionalized organizations: Formal structure as myth and ceremony. *American Journal of Sociology*, *83*(2), 340–363.

Nash, J. C. (2008). Re-thinking intersectionality. *Feminist Review*, *89*(1), 1–15. doi:10.1057/fr.2008.4.

Pietsch, B. (2020). Princeton will remove Woodrow Wilson's name from school. *New York Times*, January 27, 2020. www.nytimes.com/2020/06/27/nyregion/princeton-university-woodrow-wilson.html#:~:text=University%20trustees%20concluded%20that%20Wilson.

Purkayastha, B. (2010). Interrogating intersectionality: Contemporary globalisation and racialised gendering in the lives of highly educated south Asian Americans and their children. *Journal of Intercultural Studies*, *31*(1), 29–47. doi:10.1080/07256860903477696.

Riccucci, N. M. (2009). The pursuit of social equity in the federal government: A road less traveled. *Public Administration Review*, *69*(3), 373–382.

———. (2021). *Managing diversity in public sector workforces: Essentials of public policy and administration series* (2nd ed.). Routledge.

Svara, J. H. (1998). The politics-administration dichotomy model as aberration. *Public Administration Review*, *58*(1), 51–58.

Stivers, C. (2002). *Gender images in public administration: Legitimacy and the administrative state*. Sage Publications.

Waldo, D. (1948). *The administrative state: A study of the political theory of American public administration*. Ronald Press.

Wilson, W. (1887/2007). The study of administration. In J. M. Shafritz & A. C. Hyde (Eds.), *The classics of public administration* (6th ed.; pp. 16–27). Thomson/Wadsworth.

Yellin, E. S. (2013). *Racism in the nation's service: Government workers and the color line in Woodrow Wilson's America*. UNC Press Books.

7 Learning from the Myths of Our Past

While our field has built itself around the idea that good bureaucrats are neutral bureaucrats, that is a myth. The bureaucracy as an institution is not neutral, and as a result, the actions of individual bureaucrats are not neutral. The lack of neutrality is not necessarily a negative thing. As H. George Frederickson argued, the actions of administrators and their organizations have the potential to create injustice and inequity, but they also have the power to move toward more effectiveness, efficiency, and equity for all members of our society (Frederickson, 2010). Because of this, scholars and practitioners must constantly be vigilant and strive to pursue equity and fairness (Gooden, 2014). Moving forward, a primary concern among public administration scholars and practitioners should be to improve how we study and manage inequity in the public sector. An essential component to studying and managing inequity is understanding our history – how discussions of identity have evolved, the inequities communities have faced, and the role we have played in sustaining inequity. We encourage scholars to take a more holistic approach when studying identity by utilizing a historically grounded positionality lens.

The disparities present in communities today each have a past. They are a collection of policy and administrative decisions and actions that play a part in their existence and persistence. To address these disparities, administrators and scholars should avoid looking at a narrow slice of evidence in front of us, we must consider the broader context (Gooden, 2017). For example, "examining some data such as persisting racial inequities in homeownership while passing over other data such as the discriminatory public policies that fostered such outcomes" leads to poor decision-making from public administrators (Gooden, 2017, p. 824).

It is important we consider both the current racial gap in homeownership and the historic policies that have shaped that gap and

DOI: 10.4324/9781003322795-7

continue to shape the choices homeowners and potential homeowners have. Historically, social equity research has focused on the existence of disparities between different social groups (Gooden, 2017). In recent years, there have been several developments enhancing the ability of government agencies to evaluate their equity work (Larson, Jacob, & Butz, 2017; Blessett, Fudge, & Gaynor, 2017). However, we must make greater attempts to understand our history so we can debunk rationalized myths in our scholarship and public organizations.

We want to challenge scholars and practitioners to question their actions with respect to inequity. After you have been exposed to the history and have a deeper understanding of systems of oppression, how do you change your practices to address centuries of discrimination and inequity? Consider Asheville, North Carolina, where the city council voted in favor of reparations for the Black community. The official resolution acknowledged the city's role in oppressing the Black community, apologized for their wrongdoings, and provided several recommendations on how the city will attempt to atone for its previous actions. The actions of the Asheville city council highlight a central quality of historically grounded positionality – it is a two-step process. Historically, grounded positionality is not only learning your history, but it also involves using that information to alter your actions.

Understanding the Myths of Our Past

Rationalized myths are a threat to equity. When we believe rationalized myths, we prevent ourselves from seeing and questioning. We fail to acknowledge how our policies and procedures have consistently led to disparities and refuse to pursue equity. To address rationalized myths in our scholarship and administrative practices, public administrators and scholars need to know their history. We need to answer questions of how public administration is might be influenced by historical bias, and how our actions have impacted the lives of marginalized communities. When scholars and practitioners are knowledgeable on the field's history, they can have a deeper understanding of how public policies, administrative practices, and public sector research have reinforced and reinscribed inequities.

Myths Explored So Far

As mentioned at the start of this book, our desire to complete this project stemmed from a shared understanding that discussions of equity, identity, and discrimination often missed the mark in public administration scholarship. So much of the literature is grounded in ideals of objectivity and neutrality that often overlook the ways in which public institutions reproduce disparities and inequality.

In Chapter 2, we open our analysis with a discussion of identity in public administration. Our purpose in this chapter was to highlight the significance of understanding identity in the context of public sector organizations, while also providing a broad overview of common identity categories found in the literature. With that we explore three concepts often used to explore identity in public administration scholarship: gender, race, and heteronormativity. Gender research has focused on incorporating perspectives of women, understanding the implications of gendered norms, and conducting legal analysis that provide insights on sex-based discrimination. We then move on to discussing race. This is a topic that has recently come to the forefront of public administration scholarship, with researchers beginning to take on topics of racism, administrative racism, and critical race theory. Finally, with respect to heteronormativity, scholars studied perspectives of LGBTQ employees, organizational policies that will support LGBTQ employees, and provided reviews and analysis of legal protections of those identifying as LGBTQ.

Following our discussion of these concepts, we present frameworks that account for the multiple identities someone can possess, intersectionality and historically grounded positionality. While intersectionality has been helpful in providing public administration scholarship with a nuanced understanding of identity that moves beyond a siloed view of identity, we push for the field to begin to incorporate historically grounded positionality because it acknowledges that contextual factors that make identity situational and fluid.

Following our discussion of identity, we begin to analyze commonly held myths in the field of public administration. Reconsider the allegory of a flood from Chapter 1. The flood can represent racism, sexism, or any other form of discrimination. When that flood enters our homes, that is our public institutions, it taints everything. Even long after the flood waters have receded, the toxins left behind can continue to harm us. We tell ourselves the foundation of our house is still strong, so there is no need to look within the walls. We are scared to acknowledge that work that may need to be done to have a home that is safe. Instead, we rationalize away that extra effort needed to rid our home of these toxins. Although explicit discrimination is outlawed – the flood waters have receded – we have not adequately acknowledged all the toxins that remain. Furthermore, we have justified ignoring the toxins that remain through rationalized myths. Our central purpose in this book was to begin to address these myths, so that we can recover from the flood. To this end, we have explored three myths in the field of public administration: the myth of merit, the myth of representation, and the myth of legal remedies.

Chapter 3 opens our analysis of commonly held myths in public administration, with an exploration of the myth of merit. Our focus here was to highlight how perceptions and expectations of merit are often in flux. We have seen definitions of merit change and evolve throughout the field's history. Expanding on our discussion of identity from Chapter 2, we utilize social construction as a framework to argue that the application of merit is often based on understandings of who deserves to be a public servant – those undeserving are excluded from being viewed as in alignment with the concept of merit. While we often anticipate that deservedness is based on skill and qualifications, history shows us that deservedness is often connected with one's identity. Specifically, our focus is on how changes in expectations of merit have, at times, harmed those historically excluded from public service (i.e., women, people of color, and LGBTQ individuals) because those responsible for implementing merit-based systems viewed them as undeserving.

Following our discussion of merit, we use Chapter 4 to explore the myth of representation. Our focus in this chapter is to explore the influence of representative bureaucracy on the field of public administration. Representative bureaucracy is a foundational concept helping to shape the field's understanding of diversity and equity. However, our purpose in this chapter is to highlight how an overreliance on representative bureaucracy, as a means to understand diversity and equity, has limited our ability to understand systemic racial and gender discrimination. Specifically, we argue that primarily relying on representation (i.e., hiring diverse administrators), as a solution to longstanding issues of discrimination, avoids discussions of institutionalized behaviors and reinforced inequity, and places the burden of resolving these issues on historically marginalized groups. We conclude this chapter by highlighting the importance of holding public administrators accountable for failing to serve all citizens, clients, and employees, rather than assuming that administrators are limited in serving only those they identify with.

Finally, in Chapter 5, we explore the myth of legal remedies. Those critical of racial justice will often suggest that antidiscrimination laws and the courts prevent workplace discrimination. Furthermore, individuals in this camp may suggest that if workplace discrimination were to take place, antidiscrimination laws and the courts provide the adequate protections to resolve these issues. Our purpose in Chapter 5 is to explore the limits of this logic. Specifically, we are interested in exploring the limits of the laws as a legal remedy for discrimination. Our central aim is to highlight that the law alone does not create social or organizational change, and having antidiscrimination laws on the books does not necessarily mean we have no discrimination in practice. To this end, we explore civil rights laws in the United States relevant to workplace settings, while also providing a critique of these laws and their shortcomings in providing protections for historically marginalized groups. Our hope for this discussion is to make clear how the antidiscrimination law has limits in the protections it provides, and our lack of understanding on those limits shapes current workplace practices.

In Chapter 6, we turn our attention to the concept of historically grounded positionality. Over the past several years, public administration scholars have begun to incorporate the concept of intersectionality to gain a deeper understanding of identity in public sector organizations. While intersectionality is a valuable framework, we argue that historically grounded positionality can provide additional nuance on the complexities of identity. Because historically grounded positionality encourages scholars to look at how someone's lived experiences influences their identity, it provides additional understanding of how individuals interpret their identity.

Myths Left to Explore

While we have explored several myths present in the field of public administration throughout this text, there are still many myths left to explore.

One myth left to explore is the myth of professionalism. As we discussed in Chapter 1, professionalism was central to the development of public administration as a field of research and practice. However, when attempting to establish a professional identity for public administrators, it is important to ask ourselves if and how individual attributes were incorporated into our understanding of professionalism. Specifically, throughout this book we have argued that masculinity, whiteness, and heteronormativity were essential in the historical development of public administration of a field of research and practice. Recognizing this, it is necessary to ask how these characteristics shaped the field's professional identity, and the implications this has for people lacking these characteristics.

Consider the court case *Equal Employment Opportunity Commission v. Catastrophe Management Solutions*. This case involves Catastrophe Management Solutions (CMS) rescinding an offer of employment to a Black woman after she said that she would not be removing her dreadlocks while employed by CMS. The EEOC argued that wearing dreadlocks should be protected under race of Title VII of the Civil Rights Act of 1964 because it is often culturally associated with individuals that are Black or of African descent. However, the case was dismissed. Recognizing that discrimination based on hairstyle and texture was an issue, some states began drafting policies that would prohibit this form of bias. For instance, in 2019, California passed Senate Bill No. 188 that expands the definition of race to protect "traits historically associated with race, including but not limited to, hair texture and protective hairstyles."

This example highlights explicit action from a private sector employer to deny employment, based on the applicant's inability to meet *professional standards* of the organization. However, it is important to think about all the ways these same actions may take place implicitly within the public sector. Consider the implicit judgments made about a candidate during an interview. While nothing is said explicitly, we have to think about the implicit ways someone might be evaluated that are grounded in ideals of professionalism but may not actually be associated with someone's qualifications for a position.

Because masculinity, whiteness, and heteronormativity have historically been attached to the field's understanding of professionalism, we must ask ourselves how this may implicitly harm those lacking these attributes. For example, in a field that has grounded its professional identity in masculinity and whiteness, how does this impact the employment experiences of women and people of color? While identifying professional standards based on skill sets is necessary for the field's development, we have yet to fully acknowledge the ways non-job related attributes have been connected to professionalism throughout the field's history. Addressing the myth of professionalism is an area that scholars can explore to gain a deeper understanding of equity and diversity in public administration.

Another myth that scholars can explore is the myth of excellence versus equity. While several scholars have pushed for equity to be considered a pillar of public administration (Svara & Brunet 2004, 2005; Gooden & Portillo, 2011), this notion has often been challenged. Part of the justification for challenging the pursuit of equity is that it comes at a cost that is the reduction of excellence.

As we discuss in Chapter 3, affirmative action emerged in the 1960s during the Civil Rights Era. While affirmative action was meant to level the playing field and include women and people of color in public bureaucracies, since they had historically been excluded, it was met with resistance. The assumption of those against affirmative action was that employers were no longer going to hire the best person for the job, but the person that met expectations of equity (i.e., someone from a social group that had been historically discriminated against).

While affirmative action was developed to help historically marginalized groups by increasing their representation in public bureaucracies, it also created challenges for these groups – those against affirmative action claimed they lacked the skills to truly earn these positions. In short, by prioritizing equity, public agencies would be sacrificing excellence.

Although quotas allowing for organizations to set requirements on the hiring of historically marginalized groups were deemed unconstitutional in *Regents of the University of California v. Bakke*, the stigma around equity and hiring processes remains and is manifested into the myth of equity versus excellence. It is, of course, important to point out that even the earliest discussions of affirmative action focused on increasing opportunities for fully qualified individuals from historically marginalized backgrounds. Meaning there was never a trade-off between equity and excellence, but a recognition that many excellent candidates have been historically excluded. Better understanding the development of this myth and its lasting impact on perceptions of equity today will provide public administration scholars with nuanced insight on how to promote equity in organizational practices.

Together, the myth of professionalism and the myth of equity versus excellence highlight that we still have a long way to go in understanding the foundation of our field and its quest for equity. Future research that takes on the tasks of exploring these myths will provide nuance to discussions of identity and equity in public administration scholarship.

Historically Grounded Positionality in Public Administration

A key objective of this book has been to introduce the concept of historically grounded positionality, and make a case for why it is a concept that can be of value to public administration scholars and practitioners. As we mentioned in Chapter 6, historically grounded positionality is a framework that pushes us to acknowledge how someone's lived experience and current position influences their view of the world. Because social expectations around identity and equity evolve, historically grounded positionality provides a lens to view how these concepts are more fluid rather than static. Moving forward, it is necessary to consider how historically grounded positionality can improve the practice and scholarship of public administration.

Opportunities in Scholarship and Practice

Within public administration scholarship, historically grounded positionality can help research more accurately reflect the experiences of public servants and the communities they serve. Historically, in the field of public administration, we have used rigid understandings of identity – someone identifies as "white" or a "minority," or someone identifies as a "man/male" or a "woman/female." Furthermore, we often take these different identity categories and use them to predict outcomes and behaviors of individuals within the public sector. While these prior findings are helpful, historically grounded positionality can provide additional nuance to these understandings.

Within public administration practice, historically grounded positionality can help administrators implement policies in a more inclusive manner by taking a wholistic view of the experiences different groups have had with the public sector throughout history. Over the past few years, public agencies from all levels of government have been pushed to be more inclusive, especially toward historically marginalized groups. This will require public administrators to have a deeper understanding of the communities they serve, and their historical experiences with the public sector. Historically grounded positionality can help public servants in doing this work.

For example, in 2021, the COVID-19 vaccine was made available to people across the United States. However, there were several concerns regarding the rate at which Black communities would get vaccinated. Historically grounded positionality encourages us to understand how someone's past influences their current position from which they view the world. If consider the past experience of many Black communities during the Tuskegee experiments that spanned several decades, it provides a deeper understanding of why they might be skeptical about receiving help from the government during a public health crisis (Warren, Forrow, Hodge, & Truog, 2020). When we explore the issue of COVID vaccinations within Black communities using historically grounded positionality as a framework, we can approach the problem with understanding and empathy, and come up with solutions that better meet the needs of the community being served.

Across communities and governments, understandings of identity and equity vary. Historically grounded positionality provides a lens to explore these variations and the way they shape someone's worldview and experiences with the public sector. Scholars studying the public sector, and public administrators that serve diverse communities, must be able to recognize the ways in which lived experience and identity interact. In short, we must move past our more rigid understandings of identity and recognize the way identity changes and adapts over time and in different environmental settings. By doing this, we can begin to see the true complexity of identity and address the complexity in our scholarship and practice.

Moving Forward with Equity

Moving forward, it is important to consider how we can pursue equity by working upstream. When thinking about how to work upstream, it is helpful to consider the example of King County, Washington's efforts to address racial inequity (Valenzuela, 2017). Recognizing the disparate racial outcomes present within King County, organizational leaders, especially those in the Office of Equity and Social Justice, decided to focus their efforts on taking a proactive approach to racial inequity that involved attempting to address equity issues in their earliest states (Valenzuela, 2017). In sum, the goal of King County was to address root causes of inequity – to identify the problem upstream, rather than downstream (Gooden, 2017).

We suggest that when attempting to move forward and pursue equity, this is the approach scholars and practitioners should focus on – working upstream. Identifying the need to address equity issues in their early stages, the question then becomes: what does working upstream look like in public administration research and practice? We recommend three strategies. First, placing a greater emphasis on pursuing equity in public administration teaching and training. Second, holding those responsible for inequity accountable through more proactive means. Third, grounding public administration scholarship discourses surrounding identity that emphasize theoretical and methodological rigor.

Pursuing Equity in Public Administration Teaching

The completion of professional degree programs is a central component of socializing students into the field of public administration and creating expectations of public values that should be the center focus of their careers. If the field desires to have a public workforce that values equity, training on the significance of this topic begins during the completion of the public administration degrees.

We often tend to focus on masters-level programs when evaluating public administration and public affairs programs because there is currently not an accreditation process for undergraduate programs. However, undergraduate degree programs are an excellent place to begin professionally training students interested in public service on the values of diversity, equity, and inclusion. As of 2019, NASPAA has identified 70 programs offering undergraduate degrees in public administration or a related field. However, Sweet (1998) suggests that there are more than 160 universities offering undergraduate programs with degrees or concentrations in public affairs and administration.

Several public organizations have sought to prioritize diversity, equity, and inclusion. However, even with these efforts, there are still many recent examples of women, people of color, and LGBTQ individuals facing exclusion in their organizations. For instance, the St. Louis County Police Department was charged with discriminating against an officer that identifies as gay, following comments regarding the officer's sexuality from organizational leaders (Treisman, 2019). While issues like this may seem as though they are the sole responsibility of the individual organization, they reflect the public sector as a whole and highlight the need to train those in the public workforce on the importance of equity and inclusion. Public administration academic programs must be willing to educate to students on issues relating to diversity, equity, and inclusion, to help mitigate discriminatory behavior and assist public servants preparing to manage a diverse workforce.

Along with undergraduate students, teaching in diversity, equity, and inclusion must also span to graduate level students. Central to building a public workforce that is prepared to take on problems related to diversity, equity, and inclusion is ensuring that students are trained on these topics during the completion of their professional degrees. Currently, within the standards for accreditation, university MPA programs must ground their curriculum in NASPAA's Universal Required Competencies. With respect to diversity, equity, and inclusion, upon completion of their programs, students must be able "to communicate and interact productively with a diverse and changing workforce and citizenry" (p. 8). This required competency helps prioritize cultural competency and diversity in the trainings of public servants, but there is more that can be done. While NASPAA has a rigorous accreditation process for university programs, there is currently no requirement for NASPAA accredited programs to offer or mandate courses focused on diversity, equity, and inclusion. Requiring courses in diversity, equity, and inclusion for MPA students will be essential to ensuring their preparation in serving continuously evolving communities.

Holding Those Responsible for Inequity Accountable

In a field of research and practice that promotes democratic responsibility and professionalism, accountability is a core value in public administration. While accountability is a central tenet of the field, it remains a concept with various "meanings and dimensions" that are often context-based (Chan & Rosenbloom, 2010, p. 12S). The definition often called upon within the field of public administration comes from Romzek and Dubnick (1987), who define accountability as, "the means by which public agencies and their workers manage the diverse expectations generated within and outside the organization" (p. 228).

One means to understand inequity and accountability is using the Romzek and Dubnick (1987) accountability framework. This framework includes four types of accountability – bureaucratic, professional, legal, and political. Bureaucratic accountability emphasizes hierarchical relationships among organizational members and focusing priorities of the organization based on the direction of those at the top of the hierarchy. Professional accountability is an approach that places control with employees possessing the knowledge and expertise to guide the organizational activities being conducted. Legal accountability emphasizes the control of those outside the organization with the ability "to impose legal sanctions or assert formal contractual obligations" (Romzek & Dubnick, 1987, p. 229). Finally, political accountability indicates a public administrator's responsibility to be responsive to the interest and needs of their constituents. Based on Romzek and Dubnick's (1987) framework, bureaucratic and professional accountability depict internal control sources (i.e., organizational leaders and professional standards of employees), while legal and political accountability depict external sources of control (i.e., legal requirements and expectations of the general public and politicians).

Often, the most intensive and severe situations of inequity with respect to public management are addressed using methods of political or legal accountability. Relying on political and legal accountability is a reactive response to inequity by the organization and its members. To properly address concerns of inequity, public sector organizations must place a greater emphasis on internal mechanisms of accountability (i.e., bureaucratic and professional accountability). By prioritizing bureaucratic and professional accountability, public sector organizations and their employees can have a more proactive approach to addressing inequity.

What does prioritizing bureaucratic and professional accountability with respect to inequity look like? First, because bureaucratic accountability focuses on hierarchy and prioritizing objectives and policies of those at the top of the organization, this form of accountability would emphasize pursuing equity through expectations set at the top of the organization. Often times, prioritizing equity involves changes in organizational culture. Implementing and embedding changes in organizational culture often fall onto the shoulders of organizational leaders (Schein, 2010). Convincing other organizational members that equity should be prioritized can be a difficult task, but the greatest tool that organizational leaders and managers have to communicate the organization's values is "what they systematically pay attention to" (Schein, 2010, p. 237). Systematic attention can be established through more formal practices like rewards or data that agencies and departments are required to maintain. However, there is also opportunity for more informal practices, such as comments that managers make regarding topics on issues of equity (Schein, 2010). Regardless of the strategy being used, bureaucratic accountability emphasizes the role of organizational leaders when it comes to prioritizing equity in the public sector. By those at the top of an organization's hierarchy promoting the pursuit of equity-based values, other organizational members will hopefully prioritize equity as well.

Because professional accountability focuses on giving more control to employees because of their knowledge and expertise (Romzek & Dubnick, 1987), this form of accountability would require a greater emphasis placed on the training and education of public servants, so they can possess knowledge and expertise in diversity, equity, and inclusion. This reiterates the need for public administration and affairs programs to ensure their students complete a course focused on diversity, equity, and inclusion. However, it also highlights the need to make diversity, equity, and inclusion a cornerstone of professional organizations that help guide the values of public administrators.

Grounding Scholarship in Identity

Finally, in addition to prioritizing equity in our teaching and emphasizing accountability in practice, scholars can begin to more deeply ground their scholarship in identity. The field of public administration has conducted decades of research focused on the outcomes of different social groups as they work within and are served by public sector organizations. However, there is an opportunity to deepen this area of research and gain more insight on the concept of identity.

As we discussed in Chapter 2, identity represents how someone can be categorized and the group memberships they are allowed to align

with (Deaux, 1993). Recent scholarship highlights that identity formation is a combination of how someone perceives themselves and how
others perceive them (Headley, Wright, & Meier, 2021). This explan-
ation of identity suggests that one's identity is often more fluid than
scholars realize since identity is a function of where someone is and the
people they are interacting with.

One could argue that the area of public administration scholarship that has given identity the most attention is intersectionality. By
acknowledging the multiple identities that someone possesses and
attempting (Bearfield, 2009) to understand how this shapes someone's
interactions with the public sector, intersectionality research provides
a lens that begins to grasp the complexity of identity. However, as we
discuss in Chapter 6, it still lacks a perspective that takes into consideration the contextual and environmental elements of one's lived experience that influences their identity.

It is important that we attempt to gain a more wholistic view of
identity that better reflects the experiences of public servants and
constituents, which can be achieved through historically grounded
positionality. By recognizing the different ways someone can interpret
their identity based on the environmental context, we can refine our theoretical and empirical research on equity in the public sector.

Continuing Onward Toward Recovery

In Chapter 1, we presented an allegory from Stewart and Ray (2007)
of a community recovering from a flood. In their allegory, they equate
racism with a flood, so when the flood waters rise they enter and con-
taminate our institutions. Even when the flood water recedes, because
we have outlawed explicit forms of discrimination, we must still be cognizant of all the flood has left behind that we cannot see. While we may
no longer see the water, it does not mean that we are safe from the toxins
left behind. So, although we have several policies prohibiting discrimination, we must be cognizant of all the ways bias remains embedded in
our institutions and continues to cause harm.

As we have stated before, the remnants from the flood that
contaminates our institutions are maintained through myths. Our purpose throughout this book has been to acknowledge commonly held
myths in the field of public administration, so we can begin recovering
from the flood. While we have discussed several myths throughout the
course of this book, there are still several left to uncover. Moving forward, we hope that other scholars will continue this work. Recovering
from a flood is no easy task. It will involve questioning everything down

to our very foundations. However, this work is urgent, and it is necessary. Our hope is that scholars of public administration will take on this work, so that we can begin to recover from the flood.

Works Cited

Cases

Equal Employment Opportunity Commission v Catastrophe Management Solutions, No. 14-131482 (11th Cir. 2017).
University of California Regents v. Bakke, 438 U.S. 265, 98 S. Ct. 2733 (1978).

Literature

Bearfield, D. A. (2009). Equity at the intersection: Public administration and the study of gender. *Public Administration Review*, 69(3), 383–386.
Blessett, B., Fudge, M., & Gaynor, T. (2017). *Moving from theory to practice: An evaluative assessment of social equity approaches.* Center for Accountability and Performance.
Chan, H. S., & Rosenbloom, D. H. (2010). Four challenges to accountability in contemporary public administration: Lessons from the United States and China. *Administration & Society*, 42(1_suppl), 11S–33S.
Deaux, K. (1993). Reconstructing social identity. *Personality and Social Psychology Bulletin*, 19(1), 4–12.
Frederickson, G. (2010). *Social equity and public administration: Origins, developments, and applications.* M.E. Sharpe.
Gooden, S. (2014). *Race and social equity: A nervous area of government.* M.E. Sharpe.
———. (2017). Social equity and evidence: Insights from local government. *Public Administration Review*, 77(6), 822–828.
Gooden, S., & Portillo, S. (2011). Advancing social equity in the Minnowbrook Tradition. *Journal of Public Administration Research and Theory*, 21(11), i61–i76.
Headley, A. M., Wright, J. E., & Meier, K. J. (2021). Bureaucracy, democracy, and race: The limits of symbolic representation. *Public Administration Review*, 81(6), 1033–1043.
Humphrey, N. (2022). Gender and public service motivation: Recognizing gender as a social structure. In P. M. Shields & N. Elias (Eds.), *Handbook on gender in public administration* (pp. 243–256). Edward Elgar Publishing.
Larson, S. J., Jacob, B., & Butz, E. (2017). *Linking social equity and performance measurement: A practitioner's roadmap.* Center for Accountability and Performance.
Romzek, B. S., & Dubnick, M. J. (1987). Accountability in the public sector: Lessons from the challenger tragedy. *Public Administration Review*, 47(3), 227–238.

Schein, E. H. (2010). *Organizational culture and leadership* (4th ed.). Jossey-Bass.

Stewart, Q. T., & Ray, R. (2007). Hurricane Katrina and the race flood: Interactive lessons for quantitative research on race. *Race, Gender & Class*, *14*(1), 38–59.

Svara, J., & Brunet, J. (2005). Social equity is a pillar of public administration. *Journal of Public Affairs Education*, *11*(3), 253–258.

Svara, J. H., & Brunet, J. R. (2004). Filling in the skeletal pillar: Addressing social equity in introductory courses in public administration. *Journal of Public Affairs Education*, *10*(2), 99–109.

Sweet, D. C. (1998). Making the case of undergraduate education in public affairs and administration. *Journal of Public Affairs Education*, *4*(3), 209–214.

Treisman, R. (2019, October 30). Missouri cop who says he was told "tone down your gayness" wins discrimination case. *NPR*. www.npr.org/2019/10/30/774805535/missouri-cop-who-says-he-was-told-tone-down-your-gayness-wins-discrimination-cas.

Valenzuela, M. (2017). King County's journey in institutionalizing equity and social justice. *Public Administration Review*, *77*(6), 818–821.

Warren, R. C., Forrow, L., Hodge, D. A., & Truog, R. D. (2020). Trustworthiness before trust—Covid-19 vaccine trials and the Black community. *New England Journal of Medicine*, *383*(22), e121.

Index

For Product Safety Concerns and Information please contact our EU representative GPSR@taylorandfrancis.com Taylor & Francis Verlag GmbH, Kaufingerstraße 24, 80331 München, Germany

Printed and bound by CPI Group (UK) Ltd, Croydon, CR0 4YY
11/04/2025
01844010-0004